The Little
Black Book

The Little Black Book

THE SINGLE GIRL'S GUIDE TO
WHO, WHAT, WHERE AND WOW!

JO HEMMINGS

NEW
HOLLAND

First published in 2004 by New Holland Publishers (UK) Ltd
London • Cape Town • Sydney • Auckland

www.newhollandpublishers.com

Garfield House, 86–88 Edgware Road, London W2 2EA, United Kingdom

80 McKenzie Street, Cape Town 8001, South Africa

14 Aquatic Drive, Frenchs Forest, NSW 2086, Australia

218 Lake Road, Northcote, Auckland, New Zealand

ISBN 1 84330 703 0

Senior Editor: Kate Michell
Assistant Editor: Rose Hudson
Proofreader: Sarah Larter
Designer: Gülen Shevki
Production Controller: Joan Woodroffe
Indexer: Sue Farr

Reproduction by Pica Digital (Pte) Ltd, Singapore
Printed and bound in Singapore by Tien Wah Press (Pte) Ltd

Contents

Acknowledgements

Who should I thank in a book like this? I suppose all those guys whom either my girlfriends or I have dated and who form the basis of those key elements that make up my suggested star ratings. They vary from the one-date wonders, the blind dates, the 'my-mate-knows-the-perfect-man-for-you' date, the speed daters, the guys met at clubs, bars, work, on trains, planes and boats and those who reached dating nirvana by becoming someone special and significant in our lives. Special thanks to the handsome, sexy, polite, witty, bright and generous men, and more begrudging thanks to the arrogant, rude, scruffy, dull and mean guys. All of you have helped shape *The Little Black Book*, and all of you will hopefully allow us women to make better dating judgements about you and have a little fun along the way.

Special thanks to the team at New Holland: to Yvonne, who never stinted in her marketing and publicity drive for the book; to Rose, for being a patient and conscientious editor; and to Gülen, for designing such a discreet handbag essential!

Jo Hemmings

Introduction

*D*ating is a two-part game. Looks, voice and humour – the essential ingredients of that all-important chemistry – may be the first elements to attract us to someone, but honesty, manners, generosity and mutual goals have to materialize quickly if the relationship is to progress on a fulfilling level. It's all too easy to get distracted by how cute someone looks, or the fact that his salary is the size of David Beckham's (OK, perhaps a slight exaggeration…). Such perks can mean you're happy to overlook his bad jokes and/or *Star Trek* obsession; however, don't let yourself get swept away from reality. You must be honest enough to take a rational, objective look at the guys that you meet and date. Would you be happy with a freelance writer who earns pennies from a few jobs a year, while you're in the 30K-plus bracket? What if he wears nylon football shirts and combats when you prefer a crisp white shirt and chinos?

No guy is perfect. Life would be tedious if we were all to date mirror images of ourselves, with the same outlook on life, political opinions and musical tastes. But there are certain vital factors in assessing whether someone is suitable for you, and it's easy to overlook these when gauging whether to see someone for a second or third date.

After a first date, you can tot up your compatibility factor based on first impressions and maybe get a surprise or two along the way. That seemingly suitable prospect may just not cut the mustard as you thought he would. The one who seemed less appealing initially, however, might just have all the elements of a great time and even long-term potential. This book comes with no guarantees, but whatever happens, you'll have some fun filling it out and reading back over what you first thought, and you'll have a great book full of guys' names, addresses, phone numbers and more. It also includes the lowdown on body language, flirting, expectations, sex and much more besides. Keep it in your handbag so you can make discreet notes in the Ladies, when you get home from a date or the next day. The perfect *Little Black Book*!

Date: 16/06/04
@: Raffles Wine Bar

Name: John Smith
Job: IT Consultant
Star Sign: Taurus

	Out of 5
First Impressions: Polite, handsome. easy-going	
Height: About 6ft	
Looks: Chiselled jaw, dark hair and eyes	4
Style: Relaxed but smart	4
Voice: Softly spoken, sometimes hard to hear	2
Sense of Humour: Witty but gentle	3
Chemistry: Almost there...	3
Manners: Very polite, maybe a bit too 'careful'	3
Generosity: Very generous, but I would have liked to have bought a drink for him!	3
Body Language: Bit touchy-feely, maybe over-keen?	2
Fun: To be honest, it was a great date, but not that much fun!	2
Irritating Habits: He rubbed his chin a lot	3
See Him Again?: Yes, I think so, see what happens	2
TOTAL:	31
STAR RATING:	* * * XX

Overall Impression: He was so good-looking that it was a bit distracting, but we didn't seem to share a sense of humour. Maybe he was a bit more nervous than me!

Mobile Number:
Home Number:
Work Number:
Email:
Address:

HOW TO USE THE DATING DIARY

The Little Black Book's Dating Diary is designed to help you judge and score the compatibility between you and your date. Part fact and part fun, the star ratings help you process the mixed feelings and emotions that often accompany the first date or two and score your man on the following 10 key factors, which combine to make up the 'fanciability' of your date:

Looks
Style
Habits
Voice
Sense of Humour
Chemistry
Manners
Generosity
Body Language
Fun

In the Dating Diary, you rate your date on a score of one to five for each of these factors, based on your individual taste and overall first impressions. You also award points for how much you'd like to see him again. You can then tot up your overall score, allowing 10 points for each star rating. So if your date scores 30, he's a three-star guy; 45 and he's a 4.5-star date and so on…

While a five-star event is clearly dating nirvana, any score above three is a positive sign. Any less than three and you may want to consider seriously whether you want to see your date again. Remember, this whole exercise should be *fun*. While the key factors are those identified by psychologists as making up the chemistry and attraction between two people, it can never be an exact science, and ultimately it's your instinct and judgement that count.

Other helpful, but not key, factors are also included on each log page: height, job, star sign and so on. There is also space to record those vital contact details for your date: mobile, home and work phone numbers and email and home addresses.

Vital Qualities

Star Signs
First Impressions
Looks and Style
Habits
Voice
Sense of Humour
Chemistry
Manners
Generosity
Body Language
Fun

Star Signs

You may or may not believe in or be bothered about star sign compatibility. Although it's not vital that you and your date are astrologically compatible, it is curious how so many of us are drawn to people from a relatively small selection of star signs. If you look back on your own dating experience and friendship history (both male and female), the chances are you will find a pattern emerging and that out of, say, 20 different people, maybe just three or four star signs keep repeating themselves.

The following advice will help you identify those dates that may be a match made in heaven as well as those where you just might be heading for an astrological fall. The signs of the Zodiac fall into four elements: Earth, Fire, Air and Water. The general belief is that a relationship with someone within the same element as you, e.g. Gemini and Libra (Air) or Virgo and Capricorn (Earth) will work better than one with someone from a different group, such as Pisces and Leo (Water and Fire) or Aquarius and Taurus (Air and Earth). However, Fire and Earth signs can work well together, as can Air and Water. Fire and Water are not meant to be compatible – fire does turn water to steam, after all! – nor are Fire and Air (fire consumes air…), Earth and Water (earth dams water) and Earth and Air (which is just not very exciting, apparently!).

WHICH SIGN ARE YOU?

EARTH
TAURUS – 20TH April TO 20TH May
VIRGO – 23rd August to 22nd September
CAPRICORN – 22nd December to 19th January

FIRE
ARIES – 21st March to 19th April
LEO – 23rd July to 22nd August
SAGITTARIUS – 22nd November to 21st December

AIR ♊ ♎ ♒

GEMINI – 21st May to 20th June
LIBRA – 23rd September to 22nd October
AQUARIUS – 20th January to 18th February

WATER ♋ ♏ ♓

CANCER – 21st June to 22nd July
SCORPIO – 23rd October to 21st November
PISCES – 19th February to 20th March

Which signs are you compatible with?

Once you know your own star sign and have subtly managed to find out the sign of the guy you are dating, you can figure out just how astrologically compatible you are likely to be. While I don't suggest that you take this too seriously, you may well be surprised by how well it works.

EARTH SIGNS: Taurus, Virgo, Capricorn

Earth signs tend to be practical and concerned with material comforts and security. Looks are often important to Earth signs, as are 'grounded' people.

♉ Taurus

Most compatible with: Leo, Capricorn, Virgo, Libra and another Taurus
Least compatible with: Gemini, Sagittarius and Aquarius

♍ Virgo

Most compatible with: Pisces, Scorpio, Taurus and Capricorn
Least compatible with: Aries, Libra, Cancer, Aquarius, Leo and another Virgo

♑ Capricorn

Most compatible with: Scorpio, Aquarius, Taurus, Virgo, Leo and another Capricorn
Least compatible with: Libra, Gemini, Sagittarius and Aries

FIRE SIGNS: Aries, Leo, Sagittarius

Fire signs tend to be active, dynamic and assertive. Passionate and inspired, they are impressed by success and ambition.

♈ Aries

Most compatible with: Scorpio, Leo, Sagittarius, Libra and another Aries

Least compatible with: Cancer, Pisces, Capricorn and Virgo

♌ Leo

Most compatible with: Gemini, Aries, Libra, Taurus, Sagittarius and Capricorn

Least compatible with: Scorpio, Virgo, Aquarius and another Leo

♐ Sagittarius

Most compatible with: Aries, Leo, Gemini and another Sagittarius

Least compatible with: Capricorn, Taurus, Cancer, Aquarius, Scorpio, Libra and Pisces

AIR SIGNS: Gemini, Libra, Aquarius

Air signs are energetic and logical. A meeting of minds is often as important as someone's looks.

♊ Gemini

Most compatible with: Libra, Leo, Aquarius and Sagittarius

Least compatible with: Cancer, Capricorn, Taurus, Pisces and Scorpio

♎ Libra

Most compatible with: Aquarius, Aries, Pisces, Gemini, Leo, Scorpio and Taurus

Least compatible with: Capricorn, Cancer, Virgo and another Libra

♒ Aquarius

Most compatible with: Libra, Gemini, Capricorn and another Aquarius

Least compatible with: Scorpio, Taurus, Virgo, Leo, Sagittarius, Pisces and Cancer

WATER SIGNS: Cancer, Scorpio, Pisces

Water signs are emotional and intuitive. While they respect their own privacy – and that of others – they also love both passion and loyalty.

🦞 Cancer
Most compatible with: Pisces, Scorpio and another Cancer
Least compatible with: Sagittarius, Libra, Gemini, Virgo, Aquarius and Aries

🦂 Scorpio
Most compatible with: Pisces, Aries, Cancer, Virgo, Capricorn and Libra
Least compatible with: Gemini, Sagittarius, Leo, Aquarius and another Scorpio

🐟 Pisces
Most compatible with: Libra, Scorpio, Virgo, Cancer and another Pisces
Least compatible with: Sagittarius, Aquarius, Gemini and Aries

First Impressions

*I*t's the stuff of clichés. Your eyes meet across a crowded room. Sharp intake of breath, butterflies in your stomach, maybe even a slight stirring lower down… the quintessential symptoms of lust at first sight. Delicious and rare. However, relationships, first dates and requests for phone numbers often don't happen like this at all. You might meet in the workplace, through friends or just through chatting on a long train journey. Whichever way you first encounter a potential partner, psychologists believe that our initial impressions are formed in the first 10 seconds of meeting someone. We quickly – and often unwittingly – size someone up, taking in their clothes, style, looks, body language, height, voice, mannerisms etc., all as one package. And while our impressions may change over time, there is a certain reliability to first impressions, as they operate much more on instinct than on fact. How often have your first impressions been proved right?

Using your instinct coupled with a little knowledge about a new guy, gleaned from watching his body language and asking a few pertinent questions, will help you work out his 'score' on looks, style, voice and sense of humour. These are the key factors of chemistry or sex appeal – powerful indicators of the durability of the sexual element in any relationship.

FIRST DATE DOS AND DON'TS

♥If that cute first-time date wants to go past first base with you and pass *The Little Black Book*'s exacting standards, he ought to be displaying a decent number of the following crucial first date dos and don'ts:

Dos
Does he...

• **Smile?** – it's simple, effective and costs nothing! A miserable man is not a sexy man.

• **Listen?** – is he taking an interest in what you're saying? It's fairly fundamental if you're going to make that connection…

• **Make eye contact?** – it may seem obvious, but it shows that he's keen.

• **Make intelligent conversation?** – small talk is fine, but does he have a brain behind that brawn?

• **Laugh in the right places?** – it shows that he's listening and that he's amused by what he's hearing. Check out his laugh, too. Giggling, cackling, snorting or a Santa Claus 'ho-ho-ho' may lose their appeal pretty quickly!

• **Pay you compliments?** – a little flattery always goes down well. A barrage of cheesy chat-up lines, less so.

• **Flirt?** – done with confidence and at the right level, it's sexy and endearing.

• **Tease?** – again, a little gentle teasing shows he's relaxed and has a sense of humour. Too much and he's going to irritate you sooner rather than later.

• **Make you laugh?** – a shared sense of humour is vital if you're going to work well together (see pages 25–6).

• **Keep a little mystique?** – telling you his life story on the first date isn't always appealing. It's nicer if he holds a little back for the next time.

• **Make you feel comfortable?** – if he's making you feel relaxed, then you'll enjoy yourself that much more. Everyone's nervous on a first date, but if he can make you feel less so, then you may be on to a winner.

• **Thank you for the date?** – it's polite, and promising if accompanied by his saying that he enjoyed himself too.

Don'ts
Does he...

♥ **Whinge or moan?** – grizzling about his job, the loud music or how long it took him to get to the date is not attractive.

♥ **Talk over you or keep interrupting?** – it shows arrogance, possible disinterest and is just plain rude.

♥ **Talk about the weather?** – it's just boring…

♥ **Look bored or miserable?** – this is a date; he should be having fun even if he is a little nervous.

♥ **Flirt too much?** – he may just have one goal on his mind…

♥ **Over-tease?** – he doesn't know you well enough and it's rude.

♥ **Forget your name?** – what is he? A serial one-dater?

♥ **Seem over-eager?** – being just a little cool on a first date is the best approach.

♥ **Talk about himself all night?** – guys who are all 'me, me, me' can get extremely boring, however fascinating their lives may appear.

♥ **Talk about past relationships in detail?** – this is a date, not a counselling session.

♥ **Ask too many personal questions?** – too much, too soon can make you feel uncomfortable.

♥ **Eat with his mouth open?** – yuck…

♥ **Talk about his future with you involved?** – avoid. He needs to get a life…

Looks and Style

*L*ooks and style are inextricably linked. The most handsome man who has dressed badly, shabbily or lazily will soon seem less appealing. Equally, the less conventional head-turner will be doing himself a lot of favours if he recognizes what suits him, looks clean and smart and makes an effort on the style front.

LOOKS

♥ Looks are important: they are what form our initial impressions as to whether we fancy someone or not. Looks are not just about natural beauty, as we women know only too well; it's often a case of how confident or relaxed someone seems or whether they are well groomed or well presented. A black polo-necked jumper on an average-looking man will always look better than a beer-stained rugby shirt on a gorgeous guy.

Of course, it's easier for women to look good. There are lots of cosmetic enhancements out there to help us: hair colours, well-applied make-up, fake tan and Lycra hold-it-all-ins can make a big difference to how we look. These little aids also give us the confidence that comes from knowing that we look good and this, in turn, makes us more appealing to men.

Men do not have access to quite as many props – and those that they do have in common with us girls, such as hair dye, male cosmetics and 'lifts' in their shoes to give them a little more height, all seem a bit sad and desperate somehow. It's an unfair world, but that's the way it is. Many men don't think that they have to make any effort at all to look good, but nice teeth, good hygiene, a sexy smile, clean clothes and a little effort on the beer belly front go a long way to making a guy more appealing to women.

Somehow, most of us generally manage to find the kind of people attractive who also fancy us. It is also true that while we may not be looking for mirror images of ourselves physically, research has shown that we prefer people with similar physical characteristics to ourselves. Instinct often kicks in – unwittingly –

telling us who may be way out of our 'looks league' in whichever direction. While it's so often true that the beautiful people of this world end up with beautiful partners and the plainer people with plainer partners, there is a great deal that anyone can do to improve their lot. A freshly showered plainer man with a good haircut, a decent shave and some stylish kit is often a whole lot more appealing than an otherwise good-looking guy let down by poor dental hygiene and questionable clothes taste.

There are those who say, of course, that looks simply don't matter and that it's the person beyond their physical assets (or deficits) that matters. This is pretty much tosh. While any fulfilling relationship is undoubtedly based on much more than looks – personality, humour, friendship, kindness and so on – it's very likely that you will find that a relationship becomes frustrating sooner or later if you don't find your partner physically appealing.

STYLE

❤Style is about presentation: the way we dress and what we're wearing certainly, but more than that, it's also the way we present ourselves to other people. It's about showing our inner confidence in an outward manner. Someone who may not be dressed in cutting-edge fashion, but who looks relaxed, friendly and kind is far more appealing than the miserable-looking guy, standing rigid with folded arms in the Armani suit. It's about finding out what suits you, what makes you feel good and makes a positive statement about yourself. In this day and age, we are what we wear, like it or not.

While many European men take an almost obsessive pride in their appearance, British men let the side down all too often. Happy to date in a football strip teamed with a pair of baggy joggers and trainers that have seen better days, some men really do themselves few favours. Look around any bar, and you'll see loads of guys that look like they have thrown together their kit while blindfolded in a charity shop. Many men think that looking good, choosing clothes that match and that suit their body types is tedious and too much trouble or makes them seem vain – or worse, effeminate – and so they don't give it much thought. If only they knew the difference it makes to us. While Brad Pitt might be able to get away with mismatching tracksuit bottoms and a faded T-shirt, most guys need a little more help on the style front.

Clean fingernails, ironed clothes and gentle but not overpowering after-shave are all good signs. Taste is intensely personal and the kind of style that you find attractive may be quite different from someone else's idea of what's good. It's also about knowing what suits you. However, you'll need a little patience and compromise when taking into account a guy's fashion style when assessing this section. General cleanliness and hygiene might just have to suffice!

So, when working out whether you want to see your date again – and awarding him those precious marks out of five – I suggest that you take into account the following elements of looks and style:

Height – women tend to go for guys who are taller than themselves, but this does narrow down the options. Don't rule out going out with someone smaller than yourself. Given that there aren't quite enough 6ft 2in hunks to go round, sometimes it pays to compromise or lower your sights just a little…

Build – while it's good to date a man who looks after his body, even they come in a pleasing variety of shapes and sizes. A man who knows how to dress cleverly in order to subtly accentuate the positive and diminish the negative is often more attractive than the muscle-bound specimen who just dresses for maximum 'form an orderly queue and come and get me!' effect!

Hair – firstly, does he have any? Sadly, there's little men can do to prevent a receding hairline or loss of hair on the crown, but we live in an age where the shaven or seriously close-cropped look is both acceptable and attractive, and definitely preferable to the dreaded 'combover'. So he's got hair? Hair colour is a matter of personal preference, but beyond that a good haircut on clean, fresh-smelling hair is a definite bonus. Greying hair can look attractive too – badly dyed hair much less so.

Eyes – whatever their colour, shape or size, eyes make a big impact on us when we first meet someone. Eye contact is especially powerful – too little and he will seem disinterested; too much and he may seem scary. For more about this, check out pages 34–7.

Mouth and teeth – while full lips are supposed to show a generous nature and thinner lips a meaner one, the key here is to imagine whether you would want this guy's mouth to kiss yours and wander over your body. Good teeth and fresh breath are also must-haves here. Does he have a great smile? A man who laughs and smiles readily, lighting up his face, is good news.

Skin – not all men can be blessed with great skin, but clean, sweet-smelling, freshly shaved skin is a real bonus. A little designer stubble or a gentle tan can look good, too.

Habits

By habits, I mean the sort of potentially irritating behaviour that you *know* will drive you crazy in time and may be deeply personal to you alone. Clearly, the kind of universally bad habits outlined in 'Manners' (see page 30) are disliked by most women, as is poor personal hygiene. However, less obviously offensive habits and mannerisms can also begin to grate.

I don't want to dwell on individual bad mannerisms here – they are such a matter of personal taste – but here is one warning that might help you to recognize a potentially irritating habit. In those heady early days of dating, your new man's crooked smile or his tinkling laugh can all seem positively charming. You noticed them almost immediately and it's part of his uniqueness that makes him seem so special. Curious then, isn't it, that a few months/dates/arguments down the line, these endearing traits have turned into desperately irritating habits?

When awarding a star rating for potentially irritating habits, remember that a high score is a positive sign, not a negative one!

Voice

The pace, accent and tone of someone's voice are so often overlooked in dating books, yet voice is a key factor in attraction, and it can have a major influence on the fanciability factor of a guy. Have you ever been disappointed by that gorgeous, tall, dark and handsome hunk because the minute he opened his mouth he had a silly, squeaky voice? You might just have to hear this guy's voice a lot – phone calls, sweet nothings and maybe even the 'lurve' declaration, so make sure it's something you can live with.

Just think about the various components involved in someone's voice – and the few listed below don't even take account what someone is actually *saying*.

ACCENT

♥ Many countries have a huge variety of regional accents. In the UK we have a rich cultural heritage of accents, from the Cornish drawl to the almost Nordic-sounding extremes of Orkney and Shetland. While some accents seem to have almost universal appeal, such as a soft Irish lilt or a gentle Geordie tone, the beauty of others is in the ear of the beholder. I'm not suggesting that you become 'accentist', but it's worth thinking about those accents that 'do' it for you and those that don't. There are also foreign accents, of course – how about a sexy French or Italian accent or the harder edge of a German or Scandinavian accent? And then there are accents within accents. Most major cities have a huge variety of accents – some regional, some based on background and others that are deliberately cultivated, from 'mockney' to 'ok-yah'.

PACE

♥ The pace of someone's voice is an important ingredient in any conversation. Too little animation, and even the most exciting of topics can render you comatose. Too much garbled speech and it's hard to hear everything so it just becomes exhausting. Sports commentators are trained to vary the volume and pace of their voices to increase the dramatic effect of a football match or a horse race. One of the most important things that actors have to learn is to modulate the pitch of their voice according to their lines in order to hold the audience's attention at just the right level. Pauses in conversation can also have a dramatic effect – making a guy sound like he's really listening to you and giving a little thought to his responses. However, when the pauses are too long he may make you feel uncomfortable, bored or just boring! This is not an easy one to get right, especially as he'll probably feel a little nervous on the first date or meeting. A little compromise is called for.

TONE

❤There is massive variety in the tone and pitch of people's voices. Could you bear to date a guy whose loud, embarrassing bellow can be overheard by the entire bar? Or the guy who speaks in a barely audible whisper? Deep voices often belong to bigger people and vice versa – but not always so.

An appealing tone of voice can make people seem confident, assertive, powerful and sexy. Monotonous voices can induce sleep faster than any sedative. As with pace, any conversation can become boring very quickly indeed without tonal variety.

SPEECH 'IMPEDIMENTS'

❤I'm not sure that I really like the word 'impediment' – some more unusual voices don't really impede at all. Some speech 'problems', such as a gentle lisp, can be highly endearing. Common voice quirks include a stammer or a stutter, the soft 'r', lisping and a nasal twang. It would be a dull world if we didn't have such foibles: it's just a case of how you deal with them.

Studies have shown that while voice is an important factor in chemistry and attraction, the tone, pace and pitch of someone's voice are equally, if not more, important than the actual words being said. It sometimes pays to look beyond the merely physical attractions on the first date, and drink in the sound of that voice!

Sense of Humour

A shared sense of humour is vital. If you can't laugh together, you've got zilch chance of loving together. Trouble is, just like that GSOH so beloved of the personal ads, it's very much an individual thing. It's not just about the basic stuff like which sitcoms or comedians you both find funny, or whether he finds slapstick hilarious while you like your humour to be a little more subtle. It's a lot tougher to define than that, and it's something that either kicks in fairly quickly or probably won't kick in at all.

Think about your own sense of humour. Dry, sharp and witty or practical joke, laugh-out-loud stuff? Whatever type of humour you have, you're going to want someone to share it with. Being with someone who makes us laugh can be really sexy. Being 'laughed into bed' – even with someone whose physical attributes might not strike you as immediately sexy – is much more common than you might think. Trouble is, some guys who do have the enviable ability to make women laugh, seem to end up as the life and soul of the party, the good-for-a-laugh guy. They often end up hiding behind this image, finding it increasingly hard to show any other side of their characters, such as sensitivity or depth. These men can find it hard to sustain a relationship beyond a first date, as their reluctance to stop 'making 'em laugh' makes them seem shallow or ultimately just plain irritating.

A shared sense of humour isn't just about making each other laugh, though – it's also intrinsically involved with character and general outlook. The ability to laugh at life and not take it too seriously is a fantastic stress-buster, and it stands to reason that those guys who don't take themselves too seriously usually have a more natural sense of humour, as well as a more upbeat attitude to life. In part it's confidence, of course, but it's also that old cliché about being able to see life as a glass that is half-full rather than half-empty. If you let life's inequalities and injustices – and we all experience these from time to time – constantly get you down, then you are clearly not going to be able to relax or be much fun.

Just as the constant joke-teller may be hiding behind the façade of joviality, the man who always allows the worries of life, on whatever scale, to grind him down, may simply have forgotten the sheer joy of 'just having a laugh'.

Laughing *with* people as opposed to *at* people is also important. Sure, we can all look at someone who's ridiculously dressed and laugh at them with our mates, but it's quite another thing to laugh at people for their disabilities or anything else that they are powerless to do anything about. Guys who laugh at, or are insensitive to, those less physically fortunate than themselves are often hiding a whole host of personal insecurities and may be very hard to get to know in any meaningful way.

So, knowing that humour – along with voice and looks – are *the* essential and immediate ingredients of chemistry and the possibilities of a rewarding relationship, you can begin to piece together your *own* values in these departments. You will be going a long way towards working out whether that date is worth seeing again or not.

Chemistry

So, what *is* this magic ingredient – chemistry – that I refer to so often in *The Little Black Book*? It's not an easy concept to define. It's not as simple as just whether you fancy someone or not – it's more like a primeval attraction that seems to spring from nowhere within minutes of encountering someone. While having good chemistry is no guarantee of a successful relationship, it is one of the most essential elements of any partnership, and a relationship without any chemistry is almost certainly doomed from the start.

You can grow to love someone, you can even grow to fancy someone, but chemistry is either there from the outset or it's not. It may be a seemingly curious mixture of different elements (see page 28). It's what sometimes attracts us to bad boys and it can make even the most unsuitable of men very hard to resist once it kicks in. Chemistry can give you butterflies in the pit of your stomach, make your head spin and give you the highest of highs. It's lust at first sight and, when it happens, it can take your breath away. It's dangerous, wonderful, powerful and, frankly, it's scary, because it's hard to take control of your feelings, even if you're just about able to control what you actually *do* about them.

Another key to chemistry is pheromones, which are odourless chemicals that attract us to someone. They are detected by something called the vomeronasal organ in our noses, and studies have proved that we are attracted to guys whose pheromones indicate a different immune system to our own. This curious phenomenon has much to do with ensuring that, biologically, we are attracted to men who will help us produce the healthiest babies. We can't legislate for this, of course, but if you suddenly find yourself attracted to a guy whom you wouldn't normally fancy in a month of Sundays, it could be those pheromones at work…

You can sometimes find yourself attracted enormously to someone who defies all your preconceived ideas and expectations about what you find attractive. He may not be a conventional head-turner, but you blush at his every word and you feel anxious, wobbly and ever so slightly out of control. It happens quickly and with a passion. To hell with convention and your personal rulebook! You just want to get his clothes off and get down to it. The only trouble is, it can happen when you meet your best friend's new boyfriend, the window cleaner or your new boss. Reason *has* to kick in, or there's likely to be big trouble on the horizon! But if it happens when you meet someone unattached who is clearly attracted to you too, then harness all that delicious passion and lust and just enjoy!

Chemistry combined with other powerful feelings that exist *outside* the bedroom is the headiest cocktail in the world – and well worth hanging on to if you find it. Chemistry rarely wanes – unlike simple lust – and if you find you get on with him just as well whether you're out to dinner, with a crowd of mates or just staying in and watching TV, you may just have an enduring and enviable relationship on your hands! Controversial though this

It could be a unique combination of:

- ♥ **PHYSICAL FACTORS:** his six-pack, the back of his neck, his arms or his eyes

- ♥ **MANNERISMS:** the way he smiles, walks or moves his hands when he talks

- ♥ **PERSONALITY:** his ability to make you laugh, his consideration or certain phrases he uses

It won't be:

- ♥ The size of his bank balance

- ♥ The fact that, on paper, he fits all your 'criteria'

- ♥ Your mutual love of sailing or salsa

view is, I'm a firm believer that a good, lasting relationship can come out of that initial chemistry, even if all the other compatibility factors, such as looks, common goals and social status, aren't necessarily there. A strong and enduring sexual passion often allows us to make more compromises on other fronts, and so become less demanding out of the bedroom and more willing to go with the flow. On the other hand, if the chemistry's not there, but you get on like a house on fire, I don't think you've got a lasting relationship on your hands. What you've got is the potential for a good platonic friendship. It may be the most awesome friendship ever – but that's what it is and probably where it should remain.

Chemistry is sublimely powerful and hedonistic and if the feeling's mutual, there really isn't much to beat it. But it's highly unpredictable, very individual and you will just have to work out what makes the 'C' factor work for you…

Manners

They used to say that 'manners maketh man', and while that phrase is archaic, considerate behaviour – which is all 'manners' really means – is still pretty important when dating.

However liberated we think we are – and our independence is definitely a good thing – consideration is always attractive. Maybe we don't necessarily want a guy to pull out a chair for us when we sit down, or open a car door, or walk on the kerb side of the street, but do you want someone who eats with his mouth open, belches or farts whenever he feels like it or is arrogant and rude to the bar staff or waiters while you're on a date? I doubt it…

A guy who's considerate at the 'micro' level – asking where you fancy eating or what you want to do for the evening – is likely to be considerate at the 'macro' level. He's more likely to be honest, kind, loyal and decent. What most of us want out of any dating or relationship situation is a little respect. The bloke who talks over you, farts at random, drinks three times as fast as you or is always late for a date is just not affording you the respect you deserve.

Just as with anything in *The Little Black Book*, the sort of manners that are acceptable to you are very much a matter of personal opinion. It's important that your expectations stay realistic, but it's also essential that you have certain minimum demands. While you may be able to overlook poor manners on a first or second date – especially if you feel the guy is so cute that it just-has-to-be-worth-it – his behaviour may well begin to irritate you big time by the third or fourth date. Heed those early signs.

Generosity

enerosity *isn't* necessarily about having loads of money, but it is about having the right attitude to money – seeing it as a tool for enjoying life as well as paying for all the sensible stuff – and while some men can't afford to be too lavish, it *is* about paying your way. On a first date, a man should be attentive enough to notice when your glass is empty. Nice though it can be for him to pay for your first meal, many women feel happier 'going Dutch' (i.e., splitting the bill down the middle) on a first date. This may be simply because it seems fairer, or it may be because it avoids any heightened sexual expectations – the meal ticket scenario.

It does make things more comfortable if you and your date have similar incomes – or at least similar spending power. There can often be an imbalance of power in a relationship when one partner earns significantly more than the other. It's not necessarily that the higher earner will see the one with less disposable income as a gold-digger, but you may have different views on where to go out on a date and what to do. You don't want to seem needy while going out to the expensive restaurants that he loves – and is paying for – but neither do you want to run up a vast credit card bill. It's also to do with values. If one of you has to scrimp and save for that mini-disc player or digital camera you've been coveting and the other changes their version of the same as often as they change their underwear, it can cause resentment.

But your aim is not to take him up the aisle – this might not be long-term – you just want to check out his generosity. Just as good manners generally indicate a greater sense of consideration overall, then a generous man is usually generous in other ways. He may well have a kindness of spirit as well as of pocket, and be affectionate with his mum, loyal to his mates and kind to animals. Conversely, a mean man may show meanness of spirit too. The bottom line is, a generous man – and not one who simply flashes the cash to show off – is showing you that he values your company and your time. Any man who isn't generous on the first couple of dates definitely isn't going to improve.

Signs of a Scrooge

While The Beatles were not wrong when they sang 'money can't buy me love', there's little that's more off-putting than a mean man. You can spot the signs quickly and learn to avoid the sort who:

♥ 'politely' opens the bar door to a group of mates, thus sneakily ensuring that he's not in a position to buy the first round of drinks

♥ counts the bill to the nearest penny and never leaves a tip on the basis that the meal was expensive enough already

♥ when 'going Dutch' on a meal, splits the bill according to what he's eaten and drunk rather than going 50/50

♥ subtly guides you towards the sale items when he takes you out to choose your birthday present

♥ only ever pays for his share when buying theatre or cinema tickets

♥ walks you around for miles looking for any bar with a happy hour

Body Language

ody language consists of non-verbal gestures, postures and expressions that combine to reveal more about you and your date than mere words ever can. It speaks volumes about our attitudes, behaviour and responses, intentionally or otherwise. Whatever words we actually speak, our body language is sure to give us away if we are not being honest. The way someone walks, stands or uses their hands or their eyes can give you loud and clear messages if you learn to recognize what you are looking for. It pays to learn to read the body language of the men you meet. It is also useful to learn a little about your own body language and how to put it to good effect.

Psychologists estimate that up to 93 per cent of social interaction is communicated through body language and tone of voice, which means that the actual words we speak make up only seven per cent! Of this 93 per cent, tone of voice accounts for around 38 per cent, leaving a whopping 55 per cent of communication down to body language alone. So, a little understanding of the basics of body language would seem to be a pretty invaluable tool in your dating armoury. It enables you to interpret what your date is *really* saying to you and also helps in revealing what he might be trying to conceal.

Women tend to be more expressive in their body language and are also better at reading the signs than men. According to studies, this is because women have had less power than men traditionally, and it is the role of the less powerful to pay more attention to those with more power. While the power balance may have shifted in the last generation, we females have retained our enhanced ability to interpret body language.

CLUSTERS

♥ Body language signals work best in 'clusters', i.e. with a group of at least three or four signs working together. One or two on their own can be meaningless and will not give a positive enough indication of either interest or disinterest. While men and women do exhibit different body language signs, many of them are common to both sexes. Others are what psychologists would call 'gender specific messages': they are really only applicable to a specific sex, in part due to the differences between our bodies. While a man might suck in his beer gut to display his pecs, we would suck in our tummies to thrust out our breasts! Similar but different...

The signals of negative body language also display this cluster effect. Many are defence mechanisms that mean that someone wants the other person to back off. Others may just be the result of nerves or shyness and don't play a significant role on their own. Again, look for a group of three or four signs before taking the message on board.

Whether negative or positive, body language works best in harmony with verbal communication. What your date is saying, in association with his body language, is the biggest clue of all as to his sincerity. If he's telling you one thing and his body language indicates the opposite, he's probably got something to hide!

FIRST DATE BODY LANGUAGE

♥So, whether or not you want to see this guy again, it's certainly useful to know a little about what he thinks about you, too. If your date's potentially interested in seeing you again, he will certainly mirror your movements, gestures and body positions. He'll laugh when you laugh. He'll lean towards you. He'll sit close to you, with his legs or shoulders touching yours. He'll keep his eyes on you and give a gentle nod if he likes what you're saying. He may brush your arm or your leg or put his arm behind you on the sofa. He'll look at your lips from time to time, wondering what it would be like to kiss them. He may also look at your other bodily assets, thinking the same thing!

If he doesn't seem to do any of these things, or his eyes wander around the restaurant or bar constantly, then he may be regretting the first date. If he doesn't smile, nod or laugh at your conversation then he may not be smitten. Constant loo-visiting can be another sign of boredom – or possibly just a sign of a weak bladder! Men also demonstrate what I call 'negative grooming behaviour' – they might de-fuzz the bobbles on their sweater or pick at their nails and push down the cuticles – all in an attempt to avoid eye contact and to disguise their boredom unwittingly. Men who are disinterested also often become vague, defensive or even aggressive. They've got it wrong and they really don't like to fail or waste time. Beware, too, of the guy who is suddenly all over you like a rash. He may just be thinking that as a relationship, you might not be worth pursuing, but as a one-night-stand, you might be just fine.

Body language is critical on a first date, because this is the very time that people are on their best behaviour and out to impress. If there's a wolf in sheep's clothing underneath that smart, polite, attentive exterior it probably won't begin to show until at least date two (or even date three or four). If he's making a supreme first date effort with his hair, clothes and choice of restaurant, he's probably making a big effort in the body language and flirting stakes too. It may appear that every word that falls from your lips is fascinating and he's nodding and saying all the right stuff in all the right places. Don't be complacent – keep checking out his signals on your subsequent few dates with him to see if they change. In time you're both bound to become more relaxed, of course, but certain body language signs never lie. Boredom, disillusionment or disinterest may surface on date two or three.

So, keep an eye on those signs and see if anything changes. Any combination of two or more negative signs and it's not looking good. If these are combined with more stilted conversation or he makes an excuse to leave early as he's got so much work to do tomorrow, it's probably curtains for you. Learn to recognize the signs, react and get in there first and walk away with dignity. If he's keen but he's just tired or stressed, he'll call again.

So, what are these all-important signs I keep talking about?

Positive body language signs
Is he...

• Smiling widely, with his teeth showing?

• Looking around the room, then settling his gaze on you?

- Making lingering eye contact?

- Smoothing his clothes or his hair?

- Running his fingers through his hair?

- Mirroring your body language?

- Touching or 'brushing' you?

- Leaning in towards you or moving closer to you?

- Tilting his head to one side?

- Blinking a lot?

- Raising or lowering the tone and/or speed of his voice to match yours?

- Giving you his undivided attention and focus?

- Standing or sitting with his legs apart?

- Standing with his hands on his hips?

- Tucking one or both of his thumbs into his belt or belt loops, with his hands pointing towards his genital region?

Negative body language signs
Is he...

- Pursing his lips?

- Fidgeting or looking distracted?

- Fiddling with props, e.g. the cutlery or his lighter?

- Making napkin sculptures or shredding beer mats?

- Fiddling with his collar, tie or face?

- Making fleeting eye contact?

- Looking at the floor?

- Standing or sitting sluggishly?

- Shrugging his shoulders?

- Clenching his hands?

- Folding his arms tightly?

- Leaning or turning away from you?

- Keeping his distance?

- Tapping his foot or drumming his fingers?

- Yawning or rubbing his eyes?

- Smiling in a stretched or forced manner?

- Looking over your shoulder or avoiding your gaze?

- Shrugging his hands with his palms facing up?

- Not touching you, even 'accidentally'?

Fun

Above all, your first few dates should be *fun*. Even if you – or your date – are nervous, apprehensive or shy, it's a chance to find out more about each other, to have a laugh, to let that fantastic and overwhelming feeling of chemistry – and all that it promises – kick in. If this isn't happening for you by date two or three, then it may just be a slow-burn thing, but it's more likely that it just isn't going to happen. There's little point in dating if it *isn't* fun, after all!

You will no doubt kiss a lot of frogs along the way. There may well be cheating men, married men, men who promise to call but don't, baffling one-night-stands, boring men, arrogant men and so on, but looking for someone fun to date, and dating itself, will always enrich your life – even if it doesn't seem that way when it all ends in tears for the umpteenth time.

Do try to be open-minded and not to be too prescriptive about what you want from a man. Your last great love may have had dark floppy hair, great teeth and a body to die for, and your next love might actually turn out to be stocky and blond – *but* make you laugh and tingle when and where you least expect it. Chemistry is a curious beast, and you can find yourself fancying a man whom you may previously have considered not to be your type because he makes you laugh and feel adored, even if he appears to be somewhat lacking in the looks department. Remember that plainer men have to try harder, for obvious reasons!

So, if dating is to be fun, do not ever – well, not until date number three at the earliest – ask yourself that oh-so-loaded question 'Could I spend the rest of my life with him?'. This book is about helping you assess your *early* judgements, not the happily-ever-after sort. Men will certainly not be asking themselves that question until way further down the line, if ever. Men seem to let events overtake them, whereas we tend to like our lives orderly, neat and predictable. Think of dating as you would shopping. Buying your complete and perfect wardrobe in one hit would simply take the pleasure out of all those other retail therapy excursions. You'll choose some brilliant pieces that work well in your life for a while and some supposed bargains that you get tired of after just a few weeks. Occasionally, you'll find a fantastic purchase that becomes a wardrobe/bedroom staple for years to come and that you can't bear to part with!

Ten rules to keep those early dates fun:

- Live for the moment, not for the past or the future.

- Be relaxed and charming, and keep it light.

- Go with the flow and don't over-analyze situations.

- Don't dress like a whore or a nun – keep it simple, sexy and sassy.

- Don't discuss your date in fine detail with your mates – just give a brief résumé.

- If you enjoyed yourself, tell him so.

- If you want to see him again, text or call him.

- Don't feel pressurized into sex on the first date but don't deny yourself if you're sure that's what you want.

- If you don't want to see him again, tell him in a firm but diplomatic way. Don't just avoid his calls – men have feelings too!

- Remember, a date lasts for a few hours – not for the rest of your life.

Your
Dating
Diary

Date: _____

@: _____

Name: _____

Job: _____

Star Sign: _____

First Impressions: _____

	Out of 5
Height:	
Looks:	
Style:	
Voice:	
Sense of Humour:	
Chemistry:	
Manners:	
Generosity:	
Body Language:	
Fun:	
Irritating Habits:	
See Him Again?:	
TOTAL:	
STAR RATING:	
Overall Impression:	★ ★ ★ ★ ★

Mobile Number: _____

Home Number: _____

Work Number: _____

Email: _____

Address: _____

	Out of 5
Date:	
@:	
Name:	
Job:	
Star Sign:	
First Impressions:	
Height:	
Looks:	
Style:	
Voice:	
Sense of Humour:	
Chemistry:	
Manners:	
Generosity:	
Body Language:	
Fun:	
Irritating Habits:	
See Him Again?:	
TOTAL:	
STAR RATING:	* * * * *
Overall Impression:	

Mobile Number:
Home Number:
Work Number:
Email:
Address:

Date: _____

@: _____

Name: _____

Job: _____

Star Sign: _____

First Impressions: _____

	Out of 5
Height:	
Looks:	
Style:	
Voice:	
Sense of Humour:	
Chemistry:	
Manners:	
Generosity:	
Body Language:	
Fun:	
Irritating Habits:	
See Him Again?:	
TOTAL:	
STAR RATING:	
Overall Impression:	* * * * *

_____

_____

Mobile Number: _____

Home Number: _____

Work Number: _____

Email: _____

Address: _____

Date:

@:

Name:

Job:

Star Sign:

First Impressions:

	Out of 5
Height:	
Looks:	
Style:	
Voice:	
Sense of Humour:	
Chemistry:	
Manners:	
Generosity:	
Body Language:	
Fun:	
Irritating Habits:	
See Him Again?:	
TOTAL:	
STAR RATING:	* * * * *
Overall Impression:	

Mobile Number:

Home Number:

Work Number:

Email:

Address:

Date: _____

@: _____

Name: _____

Job: _____

Star Sign: _____

First Impressions: _____

	Out of 5
Height:	
Looks:	
Style:	
Voice:	
Sense of Humour:	
Chemistry:	
Manners:	
Generosity:	
Body Language:	
Fun:	
Irritating Habits:	
See Him Again?:	
TOTAL:	
STAR RATING:	
Overall Impression:	* * * * *

_____

_____

Mobile Number: _____

Home Number: _____

Work Number: _____

Email: _____

Address: _____

_____

Date: _____

@: _____

Name: _____

Job: _____

Star Sign: _____

	Out of 5
First Impressions:	
Height:	_____
Looks:	_____
Style:	_____
Voice:	_____
Sense of Humour:	_____
Chemistry:	_____
Manners:	_____
Generosity:	_____
Body Language:	_____
Fun:	_____
Irritating Habits:	_____
See Him Again?:	_____
TOTAL:	_____
STAR RATING:	★ ★ ★ ★ ★
Overall Impression:	

Mobile Number: _____

Home Number: _____

Work Number: _____

Email: _____

Address: _____

Date: _____
@: _____

Name: _____
Job: _____
Star Sign: _____

First Impressions: _____

	Out of 5
Height:	_____
Looks:	_____
Style:	_____
Voice:	_____
Sense of Humour:	_____
Chemistry:	_____
Manners:	_____
Generosity:	_____
Body Language:	_____
Fun:	_____
Irritating Habits:	_____
See Him Again?:	_____
TOTAL:	_____
STAR RATING:	_____
Overall Impression:	* * * * *

Mobile Number: _____
Home Number: _____
Work Number: _____
Email: _____
Address: _____

Date: _____

@: _____

Name: _____

Job: _____

Star Sign: _____

First Impressions: _____

	Out of 5
Height:	
Looks:	
Style:	
Voice:	
Sense of Humour:	
Chemistry:	
Manners:	
Generosity:	
Body Language:	
Fun:	
Irritating Habits:	
See Him Again?:	
TOTAL:	
STAR RATING:	*****
Overall Impression:	

Mobile Number: _____

Home Number: _____

Work Number: _____

Email: _____

Address: _____

Date: _____
@: _____

Name: _____
Job: _____
Star Sign: _____

First Impressions: _____

	Out of 5
Height:	_____
Looks:	_____
Style:	_____
Voice:	_____
Sense of Humour:	_____
Chemistry:	_____
Manners:	_____
Generosity:	_____
Body Language:	_____
Fun:	_____
Irritating Habits:	_____
See Him Again?:	_____
TOTAL:	
STAR RATING:	* * * * *

Overall Impression: _____
_____
_____
_____

Mobile Number: _____
Home Number: _____
Work Number: _____
Email: _____
Address: _____
_____

Date: _____

@: _____

Name: _____

Job: _____

Star Sign: _____

First Impressions: _____

	Out of 5
Height:	_____
Looks:	_____
Style:	_____
Voice:	_____
Sense of Humour:	_____
Chemistry:	_____
Manners:	_____
Generosity:	_____
Body Language:	_____
Fun:	_____
Irritating Habits:	_____
See Him Again?:	_____
TOTAL:	_____
STAR RATING:	_____
Overall Impression:	＊ ＊ ＊ ＊ ＊

Mobile Number: _____

Home Number: _____

Work Number: _____

Email: _____

Address: _____

Date: _____

@: _____

Name: _____

Job: _____

Star Sign: _____

First Impressions: _____

	Out of 5
Height:	
Looks:	
Style:	
Voice:	
Sense of Humour:	
Chemistry:	
Manners:	
Generosity:	
Body Language:	
Fun:	
Irritating Habits:	
See Him Again?:	
TOTAL:	
STAR RATING:	*****

Overall Impression: _____

_____

_____

Mobile Number: _____

Home Number: _____

Work Number: _____

Email: _____

Address: _____

Date:

@:

Name:

Job:

Star Sign:

First Impressions:

	Out of 5
Height:	
Looks:	
Style:	
Voice:	
Sense of Humour:	
Chemistry:	
Manners:	
Generosity:	
Body Language:	
Fun:	
Irritating Habits:	
See Him Again?:	
TOTAL:	
STAR RATING:	* * * * *
Overall Impression:	

Mobile Number:

Home Number:

Work Number:

Email:

Address:

Date: _____

@: _____

Name: _____

Job: _____

Star Sign: _____

First Impressions: _____

	Out of 5
Height:	_____
Looks:	_____
Style:	_____
Voice:	_____
Sense of Humour:	_____
Chemistry:	_____
Manners:	_____
Generosity:	_____
Body Language:	_____
Fun:	_____
Irritating Habits:	_____
See Him Again?:	_____
TOTAL:	_____
STAR RATING:	_____
Overall Impression:	* * * * *

_____

_____

_____

Mobile Number: _____

Home Number: _____

Work Number: _____

Email: _____

Address: _____

Date:

@:

Name:

Job:

Star Sign:

	Out of 5
First Impressions:	
Height:	
Looks:	
Style:	
Voice:	
Sense of Humour:	
Chemistry:	
Manners:	
Generosity:	
Body Language:	
Fun:	
Irritating Habits:	
See Him Again?:	
TOTAL:	
STAR RATING:	* * * * *
Overall Impression:	

Mobile Number:

Home Number:

Work Number:

Email:

Address:

Date: _____

@: _____

Name: _____

Job: _____

Star Sign: _____

First Impressions: _____

	Out of 5
Height:	
Looks:	
Style:	
Voice:	
Sense of Humour:	
Chemistry:	
Manners:	
Generosity:	
Body Language:	
Fun:	
Irritating Habits:	
See Him Again?:	
TOTAL:	
STAR RATING:	* * * * *

Overall Impression: _____

_____

_____

Mobile Number: _____

Home Number: _____

Work Number: _____

Email: _____

Address: _____

Date: _____

@: _____

Name: _____

Job: _____

Star Sign: _____

First Impressions: _____

	Out of 5
Height:	
Looks:	
Style:	
Voice:	
Sense of Humour:	
Chemistry:	
Manners:	
Generosity:	
Body Language:	
Fun:	
Irritating Habits:	
See Him Again?:	
TOTAL:	
STAR RATING:	
Overall Impression:	* * * * *

Mobile Number: _____

Home Number: _____

Work Number: _____

Email: _____

Address: _____

Date: _____

@: _____

Name: _____

Job: _____

Star Sign: _____

First Impressions:	Out of 5
Height:	_____
Looks:	_____
Style:	_____
Voice:	_____
Sense of Humour:	_____
Chemistry:	_____
Manners:	_____
Generosity:	_____
Body Language:	_____
Fun:	_____
Irritating Habits:	_____
See Him Again?:	_____
TOTAL:	_____
STAR RATING:	* * * * *

Overall Impression: _____

_____

_____

Mobile Number: _____

Home Number: _____

Work Number: _____

Email: _____

Address: _____

	Out of 5
Date:	
@:	
Name:	
Job:	
Star Sign:	
First Impressions:	
Height:	
Looks:	
Style:	
Voice:	
Sense of Humour:	
Chemistry:	
Manners:	
Generosity:	
Body Language:	
Fun:	
Irritating Habits:	
See Him Again?:	
TOTAL:	
STAR RATING:	
Overall Impression:	＊ ＊ ＊ ＊ ＊

Mobile Number:
Home Number:
Work Number:
Email:
Address:

Date: _____

@: _____

Name: _____

Job: _____

Star Sign: _____

	Out of 5
First Impressions:	
Height:	
Looks:	
Style:	
Voice:	
Sense of Humour:	
Chemistry:	
Manners:	
Generosity:	
Body Language:	
Fun:	
Irritating Habits:	
See Him Again?:	
TOTAL:	
STAR RATING:	
Overall Impression:	* * * * *

Mobile Number: _____

Home Number: _____

Work Number: _____

Email: _____

Address: _____

Date: _____
@: _____

Name: _____
Job: _____
Star Sign: _____

First Impressions: _____

	Out of 5
Height:	
Looks:	
Style:	
Voice:	
Sense of Humour:	
Chemistry:	
Manners:	
Generosity:	
Body Language:	
Fun:	
Irritating Habits:	
See Him Again?:	
TOTAL:	
STAR RATING:	* * * * *
Overall Impression:	

Mobile Number: _____
Home Number: _____
Work Number: _____
Email: _____
Address: _____

Date: _____

@: _____

Name: _____

Job: _____

Star Sign: _____

First Impressions: _____

	Out of 5
Height:	
Looks:	
Style:	
Voice:	
Sense of Humour:	
Chemistry:	
Manners:	
Generosity:	
Body Language:	
Fun:	
Irritating Habits:	
See Him Again?:	
TOTAL:	
STAR RATING:	*****
Overall Impression:	

Mobile Number: _____

Home Number: _____

Work Number: _____

Email: _____

Address: _____

Date: _____

@: _____

Name: _____

Job: _____

Star Sign: _____

First Impressions: _____

	Out of 5
Height:	
Looks:	
Style:	
Voice:	
Sense of Humour:	
Chemistry:	
Manners:	
Generosity:	
Body Language:	
Fun:	
Irritating Habits:	
See Him Again?:	
TOTAL:	
STAR RATING:	
Overall Impression:	* * * * *

Mobile Number: _____

Home Number: _____

Work Number: _____

Email: _____

Address: _____

Date: _____

@: _____

Name: _____

Job: _____

Star Sign: _____

First Impressions: _____

	Out of 5
Height:	
Looks:	
Style:	
Voice:	
Sense of Humour:	
Chemistry:	
Manners:	
Generosity:	
Body Language:	
Fun:	
Irritating Habits:	
See Him Again?:	
TOTAL:	
STAR RATING:	* * * * *

Overall Impression: _____

_____

_____

Mobile Number: _____

Home Number: _____

Work Number: _____

Email: _____

Address: _____

_____

Date: _____

@: _____

Name: _____

Job: _____

Star Sign: _____

First Impressions: _____

	Out of 5
Height:	_____
Looks:	_____
Style:	_____
Voice:	_____
Sense of Humour:	_____
Chemistry:	_____
Manners:	_____
Generosity:	_____
Body Language:	_____
Fun:	_____
Irritating Habits:	_____
See Him Again?:	_____
TOTAL:	_____
STAR RATING:	_____
Overall Impression:	* * * * *

Mobile Number: _____

Home Number: _____

Work Number: _____

Email: _____

Address: _____

Date: _____

@: _____

Name: _____

Job: _____

Star Sign: _____

First Impressions: _____

	Out of 5
Height:	
Looks:	
Style:	
Voice:	
Sense of Humour:	
Chemistry:	
Manners:	
Generosity:	
Body Language:	
Fun:	
Irritating Habits:	
See Him Again?:	
TOTAL:	
STAR RATING:	* * * * *

Overall Impression: _____

_____

_____

_____

Mobile Number: _____

Home Number: _____

Work Number: _____

Email: _____

Address: _____

Date: _____
@: _____

Name: _____
Job: _____
Star Sign: _____

First Impressions: _____

	Out of 5
Height:	
Looks:	
Style:	
Voice:	
Sense of Humour:	
Chemistry:	
Manners:	
Generosity:	
Body Language:	
Fun:	
Irritating Habits:	
See Him Again?:	
TOTAL:	
STAR RATING:	
Overall Impression:	* * * * *

Mobile Number: _____
Home Number: _____
Work Number: _____
Email: _____
Address: _____

Date: _____
@: _____

Name: _____
Job: _____
Star Sign: _____

First Impressions: _____
	Out of 5
Height:	_____
Looks:	_____
Style:	_____
Voice:	_____
Sense of Humour:	_____
Chemistry:	_____
Manners:	_____
Generosity:	_____
Body Language:	_____
Fun:	_____
Irritating Habits:	_____
See Him Again?:	_____
TOTAL:	
STAR RATING:	★ ★ ★ ★ ★

Overall Impression: _____
_____
_____
_____

Mobile Number: _____
Home Number: _____
Work Number: _____
Email: _____
Address: _____
_____

Date: _____

@: _____

Name: _____

Job: _____

Star Sign: _____

First Impressions: _____

	Out of 5
Height:	
Looks:	
Style:	
Voice:	
Sense of Humour:	
Chemistry:	
Manners:	
Generosity:	
Body Language:	
Fun:	
Irritating Habits:	
See Him Again?:	
TOTAL:	
STAR RATING:	* * * * *
Overall Impression:	

Mobile Number: _____

Home Number: _____

Work Number: _____

Email: _____

Address: _____

Date: _____

@: _____

Name: _____

Job: _____

Star Sign: _____

First Impressions: _____

	Out of 5
Height:	_____
Looks:	_____
Style:	_____
Voice:	_____
Sense of Humour:	_____
Chemistry:	_____
Manners:	_____
Generosity:	_____
Body Language:	_____
Fun:	_____
Irritating Habits:	_____
See Him Again?:	_____
TOTAL:	_____
STAR RATING:	* * * * *
Overall Impression:	

Mobile Number: _____

Home Number: _____

Work Number: _____

Email: _____

Address: _____

Date: _____

@: _____

Name: _____

Job: _____

Star Sign: _____

	Out of 5
First Impressions:	
Height:	
Looks:	
Style:	
Voice:	
Sense of Humour:	
Chemistry:	
Manners:	
Generosity:	
Body Language:	
Fun:	
Irritating Habits:	
See Him Again?:	
TOTAL:	
STAR RATING:	* * * * *
Overall Impression:	

Mobile Number: _____

Home Number: _____

Work Number: _____

Email: _____

Address: _____

Date: _____
@: _____

Name: _____
Job: _____
Star Sign: _____

First Impressions: _____

	Out of 5
Height:	_____
Looks:	_____
Style:	_____
Voice:	_____
Sense of Humour:	_____
Chemistry:	_____
Manners:	_____
Generosity:	_____
Body Language:	_____
Fun:	_____
Irritating Habits:	_____
See Him Again?:	_____
TOTAL:	_____
STAR RATING:	_____
Overall Impression:	* * * * *

_____

_____

Mobile Number: _____
Home Number: _____
Work Number: _____
Email: _____
Address: _____

	Out of 5
Date:	
@:	
Name:	
Job:	
Star Sign:	
First Impressions:	
Height:	
Looks:	
Style:	
Voice:	
Sense of Humour:	
Chemistry:	
Manners:	
Generosity:	
Body Language:	
Fun:	
Irritating Habits:	
See Him Again?:	
TOTAL:	
STAR RATING:	
Overall Impression:	*****

Mobile Number:
Home Number:
Work Number:
Email:
Address:

Dating Know-how

Meeting People
Dating Expectations
Self-Confidence
Compatibility
Flirting
Sex
Techno-Dating
Dating Websites
Books on Dating

Meeting People

Take maximum advantage of any invitation that comes your way, however dull it may seem. You could meet an interesting man at a flat-warming party, a work do or even a games evening!

Use each occasion as practice for some of those flirting skills mentioned on pages 99–103. Don't go overboard – especially with your mates' partners, as you don't want to be seen as the predatory single woman on the loose – but always make sure you look your best. Make eye contact, ask questions, smile and give compliments – to both men and women.

Never underestimate how difficult it might be to meet a guy. There are times when you'll need to be proactive – if you're in a crowded bar and you see someone cute, just smile, or hold his eyes for a moment. Don't be too scary – a woman licking her lips while pouting is unlikely to elicit much more than an invitation back to his place for a quickie. Fine, if that's what you want, though it might also elicit a good laugh from him and his mates at your expense.

Below are just some of the places that you could meet guys, but remember it could happen anywhere and at any time, however unlikely it may seem. Don't rule out the possibility of going to a speed dating event either (more of this on pages 121–3) – they can be great fun.

BARS AND PUBS

♥These can be great places to meet people, especially when crowded. You can take the long way around to the loo to get near a cute guy you've spotted, push forward to get a drink (even when it's not your round) just to get closer to him at the bar, or spill your drink accidentally-on-purpose to get his attention. If all this sounds a little too proactive for you, you can just people-watch and give a friendly smile when someone catches your eye. Try to get a conversation going on the flimsiest of bases, e.g. 'It's more crowded in here than usual' or 'Excuse me, could I just squeeze past you to get to the bar?' – they are far better opening gambits than 'Do you come here often?'! Another device that you can use to escape the crowd is to watch for when *he* goes to the loo, wait a moment or two, then make your own exit to the adjacent Ladies, just passing by him on his way out. A smile and a moment's eye contact will give him the all-clear to move in later.

PARTIES

♥ These can be the perfect meeting places. You've got every excuse to dress up to the nines and look drop-dead gorgeous and there's invariably some connection between that seriously hot guy and the host or hostess. You've got the perfect excuse to do a little detective work before you make your approach. As in the pub or bar, you can simply smile and move in there with a decent opening like 'how do you know [the host/hostess]?', 'do you live locally?' or 'what's that punch like?' – having first chucked the tell-tale contents of your own glass into the nearest plant pot, of course. Just make sure that you keep an eye out for any signs that a man is already attached – he'll either be looking over occasionally at his significant other or she'll come hurtling over, antennae on the alert, at the first sign of competition.

NIGHTCLUBS

♥ Blaring music and subdued lighting mean that clubs are traditionally meeting places for bodies rather than minds. As a result, clubbing can be quite daunting if you want to have a deeper conversation than 'do you fancy a drink/dance?'. However, they are great places if you want to see what a guy looks like when he's dancing. A girlfriend of mine swears blind that a cool dancer will be a hot lover – all that being in tune with himself, rhythm and so on. Given the constraints of conversation, make sure that if you do meet someone you fancy, either take *their* number and give them a call or just pass on your email, mobile or work number only. Don't hand out your home phone number to anyone you don't feel completely at ease with and *definitely* don't give them your home address on a first meeting. A club can be a Mecca for weirdos and stalkers.

SOMEONE WHO KNOWS SOMEONE...

♥ There are times when a friend knows someone who might be 'just perfect' for you or knows someone who knows someone of the same ilk. This can be a quagmire of raised hopes and dashed expectations. He will either be someone just like your last love or the total opposite (and therefore probably deeply unfanciable), or someone who's been single so long that he's desperate to be fixed up and tragically rusty at the dating game. But, on the other hand, at least he will have been vetted by someone close to you, so it's definitely worth a try. However, do try to keep your expectations firmly nailed to the mast, however highly recommended he is.

DINNER PARTIES

♥ Dinner parties can be a bit like the above, and are definitely more successful if there's a good mix of people there so that you and *he* are not the only singles round the table. Otherwise, you run the risk that all eyes will be upon you watching how you're reacting to each other, and that can be a killer start to any potential new relationship – however gorgeous he may be. And if he *does* turn out to be gorgeous, do give off some subtle signals indicating that further attention (away from prying eyes) could be welcome, but don't make it so obvious that the whole dinner party can see your every move. Try discreetly passing your business card or mobile number to him and then just concentrate on chatting to the rest of the guests at the table.

WORK

♥ More than half of all long-term couples meet at work, which isn't that surprising when you take into account just how much time we spend there. You get to see someone as they actually are, without the influence of alcohol or surrounded by their mates, and observe how they operate under pressure or when dealing with clients or customers. Like what you see? Quickest way from A to Z is to ask them about their weekend on a Monday morning. Anyone whose reply begins with a 'We' is probably best not pursued. Alternatively, check out their status with another work colleague, but make sure that they have your interests at heart and won't go running straight to him with tales of 'guess who fancies you?'. You could try organizing group drinks after work or try that trusty old ruse 'I've got two tickets to a gig/play/comedy show and my flatmate can't come…'

INTERNET DATING

♥ There's more on this on pages 112–117, and there's a lot to be said for this new world of virtual dating. More than a million people regularly log on to Internet dating sites, and that number is growing rapidly. Choose a reputable site, put up a good photo of yourself, register all your details and for a reasonable monthly sum you can trawl through hundreds of eligible men online.

A word of warning, though – not all the men are quite what they seem. Some are married, others older than stated or simply fatter or balder than their 10-year-old photo implies. Some are just looking for sex. Some are desperate to get married and have kids. Some simply get off on chatting online and disappear when a meeting is suggested or, worse still, make an arrangement and then don't bother to turn up. Always chat to prospective dates on the phone before meeting, as their manner and voice are important clues as to what sort of person they are, and *always* meet them in a public place, where you can make your excuses and leave if you feel uncomfortable in any way. The same applies to meeting men through the personal or 'lonely heart' ads, introduction agencies or any other kind of 'arranged' dating. Experience and instinct will help to guide you in the right direction.

THE CHANCE MEETING

♥ You could meet someone in a supermarket (some even hold singles shopping nights these days!), a library, on the 08.34 train to work, in a record or book store (remember *Notting Hill*?), at a night class, in an art gallery, while out jogging, on a plane, on holiday or even at the launderette. It's often hard to think of something to say under these circumstances, so if in doubt, a simple 'Have you got the time?' or 'Do you know which aisle the cereals are in?' (if appropriate!) will buy you a moment of his time.

In supermarkets, you can tell a lot by looking inside a man's basket or trolley. Baby food and sanitary towels are a bit of a giveaway, as are microwave meals for one and frozen oven chips!

FIRST DATE SUGGESTIONS

♥OK, so you've met, you've hooked up and now you're clearly going to have to go somewhere on your first date – in order to fill the pages of *The Little Black Book* if nothing else!

Favourite venues are bars or restaurants, for obvious reasons. He may come up with an innovative idea that proves his alpha male creativity! If you're shy or nervous, it's often good to have a first date at the movies, the theatre or even a football match – it'll give you something to talk about afterwards, over a drink, if either of you are feeling a bit tongue-tied. Here are some other suggestions to consider, depending of course on the time of year, the weather etc.:

- ♥ A walk in the park, followed by a drink or a bite to eat

- ♥ A trip to the movies, theatre, jazz club or comedy club

- ♥ Clubbing

- ♥ An activity such as bowling, roller-blading or ice skating

- ♥ Greyhound or horse racing

- ♥ A day trip to the seaside

- ♥ Boating on the river and a picnic

- ♥ A trip to a theme park or fun fair

- ♥ A game of tennis or badminton

- ♥ A trip to an art gallery, museum or exhibition

- ♥ Lunch in a country pub

Dating Expectations

he 'Perfect Man' *doesn't exist*. And if he did and he were mine, I'd live in a permanent state of frayed nerves, worried that the moment he stepped out of the front door it would be straight into the arms of a taller, leggier, slimmer and bigger-breasted specimen than myself. I'd have to keep him under lock and key and bring him out for special occasions only, preferably under cover of darkness and to male-only gatherings.

While it's dangerous to go searching for the 'Perfect Man', it *is* wise to have a few realistic expectations from the outset, otherwise you've got no parameters to work within. By expectations, I mean a sort of a 'wish list' of the kind of qualities that you'd ideally like your man to have. This is bound to include a few physical factors such as preferred build, height and possibly hair and eye colour, but try not to make these too precise or you'll miss out on dating opportunities because men simply don't fulfil your demanding criteria. Going for a 6ft-tall, blue-eyed Adonis with dark, floppy hair will certainly focus the search, but might just narrow the field down to a barren one. You also might meet someone who fulfils your physical criteria, but turns out to have zero personality.

If you're too in love with finding 'The Perfect Man', then you're just being too picky. Be open-minded and try to stay realistic, or you will simply find that your overly high expectations will yield disappointing results. Keeping certain standards is critical to self-esteem, but going too far in the search for perfection will inevitably leave you disappointed and dateless. Consider the average man's simplistic idea of a perfect woman. You've got it – tall, blonde and busty – or a subtle variation on that theme!

LOVE AT FIRST SIGHT

❤ Sorry if this sounds negative, but it just ain't possible. Longing, lust, desire: maybe. But love: never! It is possible to know that you could have the capacity to love someone after a date or two, but it can't flourish into anything lasting for some time after that. Dating is a double-edged sword, and lurking behind that gorgeous façade could be a seriously unattractive person. As you get to know someone, you will experience both the good and the bad. He may be all that you wanted in a man, but the more time you spend getting to know each other, certain traits, personal habits and behaviour will invariably surface that you may grow to love, but wouldn't be on your initial wish list. That's just life.

YOUR WISH LIST

❤Dividing your desires and expectations into two sections: 'must-have' and 'would-like-if-possible-but-accept-it-might-just-be-a-bonus' is a useful exercise. The 'must-haves' would include 'is solvent', 'lives within easy distance of me', etc. and the 'would-likes' might include that man with dark, floppy hair (a recurrent theme, I know, no prizes for guessing why…) or having a similar career or common hobby. Inject a little compromise into your wish list and you'll have lots more fun along the way. Focus on just a few of the really critical dating variables and make an effort to overlook the others. Keep refining that list and avoid becoming a snob or a gold digger. The more people you date, the better you'll get at dating.

These are some of the factors that you might want to consider:

- ❤ Do you want him to be your best friend as well as your partner?

- ❤ Do you want to be able to laugh at the same things?

- ❤ Are you looking for long-term commitment or something else? Is he looking for the same thing?

- ❤ If you are looking for commitment and want a family at some time, could you imagine having his babies?

- ❤ What level of independence do you want to retain or are you looking for a 24/7 togetherness?

• Is it important to you that your libidos match?

• Could you cope with, or do you actively want, a relationship where monogamy is not a prerequisite?

• Do you want or expect complete devotion, or would a jealous man send you heading for the hills?

• Do you admire ruthless ambition and drive in a man, or would you prefer someone who just goes with the flow?

• Do you want or need someone on your intellectual or social level?

• Do you want someone close to your own age or would an older or younger man appeal to you?

• Is instant chemistry critical or do you believe that it can develop over time?

• Do you mind or want a smoker? A drinker? Or a gym/fitness junkie?

BE REALISTIC ABOUT YOURSELF

♥ Tough though it can be, it's an invaluable exercise to stand back and take an honest look at *yourself*. How desirable are you? How attractive or appealing are you to men? What kind of man is likely to go for *you*? It's worth drafting in the help of someone that you respect and whose opinion you both value and trust to help you with this. This could be a really close girlfriend; a close male friend would be even better (especially if you're in the fortunate but rare position of still being mates with an ex, whom you still like, trust and respect). A word of caution, though: if either of you is secretly hoping to woo the other back, this exercise will not work!

You'll need to ask them a series of questions. Be prepared for answers you might not want or expect. Try some of these for size:

- Do you think I'm attractive to men?

- How would you rate my attractiveness on a scale of one to 10?

- What could I do to improve my rating?

- Do you think I'm sexy?

- How would you rate my sexiness on a scale of one to 10?

- Am I a fun person to be with?

- Do I seem outgoing or shy?

- Do I dress well?

- Do my clothes suit me?

- Am I bright, well-read and interesting?

- Do I flirt with men?

- Do I flirt too much or too little?

- When I'm talking to men do I seem too interested or too aloof?

- Do I seem relaxed when I meet a guy or am I too scary?

- Am I too full-on or too passive?

You get the drift. It will not always be a pleasant experience, but you might find that it helps you to see things from a different perspective. If the responses are exactly what you expected, then try someone else, because they're probably just saying what they think you want them to say. This is meant to be a 'cruel to be kind' exercise, not a mutual back-scratching – or back-stabbing – event. However, if the answers are too harsh it's probably time to change your mates!

Ask yourself the following questions, too – it will help you see what you have to offer a potential partner...

Are you realistic in what you're looking for? – Being too demanding or narrow in your expectations will not only bring disappointment, it may also explain why you may have trouble dating in the first place. Take a little time to look beyond a guy's bank balance or his looks, and you may be pleasantly surprised by what you find.

Are you good company? – How are your conversational skills? Do you read a daily paper or watch the news, or is your cultural intake restricted to the soaps? Are you passionate about a hobby or your work, and can you convey this in a relaxed manner? Do you ask questions because you have a genuine interest in someone else or simply because you want to size them up? Do you listen well or do you interrupt and butt in all the time with your views?

Are you financially independent? – You don't have to be rich or flash with your cash, but managing your money wisely gives you confidence and allows you to see your date as a person rather than a meal ticket. Dating a wealthy man is great, but see it as a bonus rather than a goal. If a man thinks you are after him for his money, he will be guarded from the start.

Are you emotionally independent? – Do you have goals and aspirations that are your own? Goals that are not just finding a guy to be with, but goals for yourself – learning a foreign language, becoming the boss or running the marathon? These goals are not the same thing as having hobbies – these are major aspirations that you want to aim and work for. Having them shows ambition and drive as well as independence, and is often very attractive to men as well as ultimately fulfilling for you as a person.

Do you live for the present? – While looking to the future and making plans is an essential part of life, dreamy people who always think the grass is greener just around the corner do not make for good company. Enjoying today and taking life one step at a time can make you a much more relaxed person. Just think how good you feel when you're on holiday. Dwelling too much on your emotional past can make you cynical, mistrustful and just allows anyone who had the ability to hurt you in the past to carry right on hurting you in the present. Put it behind you – it's time to move on.

Are you a positive person? – Are you happy with your self-image? Are you an optimist or a pessimist? Do you grizzle and whine or tackle your problems head on, one at a time? Happiness and healthy self-esteem are infectious and make people want to become part of your life. Negative people create just the opposite effect. Work out what makes you happy and go for it. Accept compliments with good grace and a smile, not suspicion or a quick 'Thanks, but…'. Learn to recognize your strengths and work on your weaknesses.

Self-Confidence

The old cliché that we need to 'learn to love ourselves before others can love us' is never truer than when we are dating. Feeling good about ourselves is vital to success and happiness in any relationship. Our levels of self-confidence and self-esteem vary throughout our lives and, while the truly shy among us have a tougher time than most when dating, even people brimming with confidence experience self-doubt and first-date nerves.

IMPROVING YOUR OWN LEVEL OF CONFIDENCE

♥ If you can answer 'yes' to at least 10 of the following questions, then you are probably reasonably self-confident. Any less than seven positive responses and it's time to take a closer look at what is holding you back in learning to be happy in yourself. Try to be honest and answer what you believe *most* of the time, rather than *all* the time. And don't say 'yes' simply because that's what you'd like to be, rather than how you actually feel.

♥ Do you like yourself as a person?

♥ Do you think you deserve to be loved?

♥ Do you think you deserve to be happy?

♥ Have you something worth giving to someone else (emotionally, that is)?

♥ Do you feel you're basically a decent, caring person?

♥ Are you generally optimistic about life?

♥ Do you feel that your opinions matter even if they seem to be different from other people's?

- When you do well, are you proud of your achievements?

- Can you express yourself with ease in company?

- Do you find it relatively easy to say 'no'?

- Do you tackle problems individually, so they don't stack up?

- Can you take constructive criticism?

- Do you manage to control your anger or temper?

- Do you find it easy to make good friends?

- Do you take risks willingly, knowing that making mistakes is an essential part of moving forward?

Having a healthy level of self-esteem is not something that we are born with. It is something that develops over time and needs to be nurtured. It is intrinsically involved in our families, education, work and relationship history. It is also not a 'fixed asset' – it can fluctuate over the years, depending on how life is treating us at any given time. However, just as some people are naturally extroverted or introverted, optimistic or pessimistic, we have a general predisposition to having a positive attitude to ourselves – a healthy level of self-esteem – or a more negative attitude, which requires a greater struggle to learn to love ourselves.

GIVING YOURSELF TIME AND SPACE

People with low levels of confidence are often constantly busy – they arrange their lives that way. They need to be doing something or seeing people on an almost non-stop basis, because essentially they don't feel happy or relaxed in their own company. Doing nothing is not a concept that they want any part of.

If you recognize elements of your own life in this, take a little time out to be on your own. Stay in for the night, switch your mobile and TV off, put your feet up and just relax. Make yourself do this for half an hour at least three times a week. It may feel strange at first, but after a few weeks, you will learn to love that time and space you have given yourself and will have learnt, most importantly, that you actually *deserve* it.

THINK POSITIVE

♥ However low your confidence or self-esteem may be, there will certainly be things about you that you feel are at least 'not too bad'. Some of these could be physical characteristics such as nice hair, good skin or slim legs. And you can improve these things, too, by taking a visit to the hairdresser, going on a diet or taking regular exercise. Even simple things like having a manicure or buying some sexy new underwear can make you feel good about yourself. The more confident among us are not necessarily born slimmer or more attractive than those with less confidence: they just spend a little time working on their appearance to bring out the best in themselves.

Although it's often harder to work on non-physical characteristics than on your appearance, try to accentuate the positive, rather than dwelling on the negative, and make improvements to aspects of your life that you are not as happy about. Rather than dwell on all the bad parts of a past relationship, for example, try to remember the good times. If you've had yet another bad day at work, it may well be time to think about changing jobs. However, it could be that your negative attitude is making you only recall the bad bits about your day and that there were actually some good bits, too! What were they? Write them down if it helps, so that you can take a look at the list another time and remind yourself to adopt a more positive attitude to life.

Also remind yourself of important positive factors in your character that can be easily overlooked. Are you a generous person? Loyal? Caring? Reliable? Witty? A good listener? Each one of us has something to offer that can be enjoyed and appreciated by someone else. Learning to recognize these qualities is a major step towards becoming more confident. If you learn to value yourself, it makes it much easier for others to value you, too.

NATURAL SELF-CONFIDENCE

♥ Self-confident people seem to have all the fun. Throw them into any social situation, however new or bizarre, and up they pop smiling, witty, ready with the right words at the right time. Don't you just hate 'em?! Do you wonder what they've got that you haven't and where you can get some?

You might find it reassuring to know that even supremely self-confident people are not confident *all* the time. Just like shyness, confidence can fluctuate depending on the circumstances. Being dumped, losing your job or just having situations backfiring unexpectedly can be real killers even for confident people. The point about learning to be more confident is recognizing that these setbacks happen to everyone from time to time – the only difference being that confident people bounce back from them that much more quickly – and learn from them in the process.

It's all too easy to compare yourself unfavourably to that gorgeous girl at the gym, the work colleague who always seems to come up smelling of roses or the new woman in your ex's life. You must learn to look at the positive side, the achievements that you have made and those that you can make in the future. Set yourself goals, however small, and think 'I can', 'I will' and 'I'll try it' rather than 'I can't', 'Maybe I should have' or 'It's too difficult for me'. If you think you can't do something, then the chances are you won't be able to. If you think there's even a possibility that you can, then you stand a much better chance of success. And even if you don't succeed, you can try again or dump the thought and at least you'll have learned something about yourself for next time.

TEN KEY QUALITIES OF
SELF-CONFIDENT PEOPLE

♥ Self-confident people have 10 main qualities. These seem to be common for both men and women and all of them can be yours, too, with a little work and a little practice. If you feel you need to develop your confidence, especially to enhance your dating potential, try adopting some of the principles overleaf and make them work for you:

• Self-confident people learn from their mistakes, move on and don't dwell on the past.

• They take risks and make calculated decisions, knowing that even if they're wrong, the results will provide an insight into future risk-taking and decision-making.

• They take up as many new social opportunities as possible.

• They have a well-honed understanding of how they can look their best to feel good about themselves.

• They tend to be optimistic – believing that the proverbial glass is half-full rather than half-empty.

• They dump emotional baggage as soon as possible and move on without pre-conceived ideas.

• They believe that life is what you make it and that anything's possible within reason – they are in control of life rather than letting life control them.

• They also have realistic expectations about life – it isn't always what it's cracked up to be, but that's fine by them.

• They are adept and free at both giving and receiving compliments.

• They understand and feel comfortable with their own individuality, even if their style appears a little non-conformist or unorthodox to others!

TEN TIPS FOR OVERCOMING SHYNESS

♥Shyness can be socially crippling. Why does it seem that everyone else has something witty to say while you feel tongue-tied, and when you do manage to say something it never sounds as sharp or clever as you intended or simply comes out the wrong way? A bonus for shy people is that they are often good listeners – or they certainly appear to be. They also often come over as enigmatic or intriguing. Some guys relish the challenge of shy girls – too much confidence can be scary and off-putting at times.

♥ Don't think of yourself as shy – it can have negative connotations. Think of yourself as quiet or a good listener instead.

♥ Don't forget those things that you are good at and interested in. Having passions in life is a great thing!

♥ Smile, look up and make eye contact.

♥ Compliment people and accept compliments with a smile and a thank you.

♥ Don't beat yourself up over shyness – almost all of us experience it at one time or another.

♥ Notice what happens when you are more open, friendly and approachable, and enjoy it.

♥ Mentally practise awkward situations and try out a pleasant comment or two before you go out and see how it feels with a real person!

♥ Make small talk as often as possible by chatting to shop assistants, the postman and work colleagues.

♥ Have a drink before a date – a glass of wine will make you feel more relaxed – but don't have too much or you will be slurring your words!

♥ Make sure you look your best so that you feel comfortable and relaxed in yourself. Wear killer heels, have your hair highlighted or whatever is your style. Looking good makes us feel good.

SEXUAL SELF-CONFIDENCE

♥One of the reasons why we feel sexier and enjoy lovemaking more as we get older is the higher levels of self-esteem and self-confidence that we often develop as we move out of our teens and twenties. As well as feeling more relaxed in bed, we are more willing to try out new positions and places to make love. Sexual self-confidence allows us to feel lust and passion and be proactive about making sure that we get what we want; we know we can make our partner feel good, and how to do it. Confidence also helps us feel less stressed and anxious about life in general and both stress and anxiety can be passion-killers in the bedroom. If you worry less about the way your own body looks, you are free to indulge yourself sexually because you enjoy it and you know you deserve it. Having self-confidence makes hedonists and pleasure-seekers out of us all, and sex is one of the areas in life where the pleasure principle is vital to maximum enjoyment.

Sexiness comes from within. Being sexy is not simply about how much cleavage you are showing or wearing a pair of killer heels on your shapely legs. Truly sexy people can still look hot in an old jumper and baggy jeans, just as those with less conventional sex appeal can end up looking cheap when they wear revealing clothes, rather than the sexy sirens they intended. People who feel comfortable and happy in themselves tend to be more relaxed, natural and laugh more, which can be incredibly sexy even if they are not conventional beauties. The combination of pride and care in your appearance, natural and unforced behaviour and feeling at ease with your personality and your body is a heady and sexy cocktail. It's also true that most sexy women have the confidence to *know* that they are sexy and how best to use it.

Compatibility

What makes us compatible with someone else? What makes one guy so right for us while another is so obviously wrong? Much of *The Little Black Book* is about recognizing the earliest essential ingredients of compatibility – chemistry, looks, voice and humour. Should your date manage to earn himself an initially promising star rating, how can you tell whether this might lead to something seriously special further down the line?

HOW COMPATIBLE ARE YOU?

♥ Compatibility is more than simply having interests and friends in common. There are certain fundamental issues, whether we are aware of them or not, which dictate whether or not someone is a suitable match. These include our culture, interests, political views, class, religion, education, career choice, background and income level. While we may not be actively seeking partners who are mirror images of ourselves, it is certainly easier to form a successful relationship with someone with whom you share at least a little common ground.

Unless you are genuinely ready, willing and able to compromise – or your partner is – then a lack of common ground is likely to impact as the initial lust wears off. Serious incompatibility will often show up early in a relationship – if you hate swearing, prejudice, ethnic food, smoking or clubbing, for example, and your date exhibits any of these tendencies, then you're going to recognize that you are fundamentally incompatible pretty quickly. So if politics are important to you and you couldn't possibly consider dating someone who's ever voted Tory, then find out his sympathies early on. Ditto if you loathe smoking and couldn't bear to kiss a smoker.

If all these basics slot into place, the next level of potential incompatibility often reveals itself a few weeks into a new relationship. When you first start dating a new guy, it's natural that you'll both want to make a good impression on each other. So he buys you dinner, flowers and jewellery when the mood takes him, but don't expect this to last forever. After a few weeks, people inevitably slip into what I call 'normal complacency'. They relax into the relationship and a different, less compatible person may begin to emerge.

Signs of incompatibility

❤ He used to buy you dinner, send you flowers and ring constantly, but now he has stopped being so attentive.

❤ He was punctual and would always text or phone you to say if he was going to be a little late, but now he's always late and he rarely lets you know.

❤ His once clean and tidy flat has become a cesspit of empty beer bottles, take-away cartons and unwashed underwear.

❤ The car door that was opened for you has become a thing of the past.

❤ His moderate – and impressive – drinking of carefully chosen white wine has become a regular six pints of beer.

These are just examples of 'normal complacency' and there will be many others. While some may bother you and make you question your relationship, others are less worrying and an inevitable result of relaxing into a relationship. Always remember that you'll be showing similar signs too! However, once you've managed to get through the first month or two and nothing startlingly untoward has happened, life will seem a lot more relaxed. It might not indicate a lifetime of compatibility – that can take years – but at least you're probably not in for any major incompatibility surprises.

A COMPATIBILITY TEST

❤ Think about the following statements. They will help you to find out whether you're likely to go the compatibility distance with your new man. These points are (in no special order of priority) some of the common goals that bind people beyond the initial stages of a relationship. It is important to share at least half of these, if you want to go beyond first dating base:

- I want/don't want children.

- I mind/don't mind dating a man who already has children.

- Looks are/are not that important to me.

- I have a high/low sex drive.

- It's important/not important that we share political views.

- I would like/am not bothered about dating someone with the same religious or spiritual beliefs as me.

- I love/am not bothered about dining out.

- I like/hate/don't mind smoking.

- I like/hate/don't mind drinking.

- I am/am not a party animal.

- I am/am not ambitious.

- Household chores should be/don't need to be shared.

- I believe/don't believe in fidelity.

- I'm looking for/not looking for long-term commitment at the moment.

- I would like/am not bothered about being with someone who has achieved the same level of education as me.

- I like/don't like/don't mind tattoos or piercings.

- I like/don't like the outdoor life.

- It's important/not important to me that someone shares my hobbies and interests.

- I prefer going out/staying in.

- I want someone who is/is not romantic.

- I want a man who is/is not practical.

- I like/don't like spontaneity or surprises.

Flirting

So, what is flirting? First and foremost, flirting is fun. It's about making people feel good – and that means both the 'flirter' and the flirtee'. It's about giving compliments and making someone feel special. It makes people smile and feel relaxed and allows us to relate to one another.

A couple of glasses of your preferred tipple and you feel confident, upbeat and playful. Too many and you lose control, become garrulous and loose-tongued and may come to regret what you've said. And so it is with flirting – indulge in a little well-applied, well-judged flirting and you'll have a ball. Too much OTT schmoozing and cheesy chat-up lines and you'll both end up feeling embarrassed!

Flirting can, unfortunately, suffer a bad press sometimes. It is *not* about leading people on or playing mind games. It doesn't mean that you're after a quick fumble between the sheets any more than a committed life-long relationship. You can flirt at work, at a party or even with your friend's dad. It doesn't have to be sexual, aggressive or played out in a dumb or ditsy way. It's not about fluttering your eyelashes and draping yourself all over the nearest piece of male totty. Nor is it about leaving your intelligence tucked up indoors before you venture out – quite the contrary. Good flirts use their brain, their wit and their intuition.

THE JOY OF FLIRTING

♥Flirting is a terrific form of communication. To some lucky women it comes quite naturally, but in others it has to be learnt. It needs to be performed with care and common sense – a flirty man can be seen as an infidel or a lech; a flirty woman is often seen as vacuous, flighty and a tease. It's all a question of how you flirt, at what level and with whom. A woman who comes on seriously strong, in sexual flirt mode, to a married man is judging her flirt tactics badly. A man who delivers a torrent of sexual innuendo with eyes firmly fixed on your D-cup is not so much a flirt as a pain in the rear! Get the levels wrong and you just come over as sad. Get them right and you can have a ball, making someone else feel great too. Learn to gauge the situation, use your instinct and remember that when it comes to flirting, less is often more…

FLIRT MODE OR FRIEND MODE?

♥ It's not always easy to distinguish between the two, especially when you meet someone new. Of course we know when someone is littering their conversation with sexual references and silly chat up lines, while their eyes linger on the parts of your body where their hands would clearly like to follow. But that's more clumsy social interaction than flirting. Good flirting can be so subtle that it's easy to mistake for friendliness. For a reserved person, just making polite small talk could be their idea of flirtation, whereas a more confident man might hold your eyes for a moment, brush your arm, smile sexily and then excuse himself back to his gay partner on the other side of the room. Confusing, isn't it?

Often it's a case of actions speaking louder than words, so you need to take note of a man's body language or what psychologists proudly call 'non-verbal communication'. There are three instant non-verbal factors that quickly reveal whether someone is flirting rather than just being friendly. And, as well as using them to spot whether someone is interested in *you*, you can use these techniques yourself when you want to let someone know that you are interested in *them*:

Lingering, direct eye contact – if he looks at you directly in the eye for more than a few seconds – he's interested. I'm not suggesting that you actually time this, but if you feel just a tad uncomfortable, feel the need to avert your gaze to break the moment, or feel the first signs of fluttering sexual awakening, he's definitely flirting with you.

He imitates your behaviour – if he tips his head to one side when you do, smiles in direct response to your smile, leans forward when you're leaning forward or draws on his cigarette or sips his drink as you do – he's interested.

He looks at your mouth – the mouth is one of the most sensual parts of the body, being responsible for expressing emotion (as in a smile or a frown), the first physical encounter (as in a kiss), and further physical intimacy (as in taste, licking, sucking and so on). You get the picture! If he looks from your eyes to your mouth, lingers there, and then returns his gaze to your eyes, he's definitely flirting and probably keen. Watch his pupils – if they enlarge, he's finding you sexy…

GRABBING HIS ATTENTION

♥ OK, so you want to get noticed and flirt with him, but you aren't quite ready to make the first move. Just looking like you're having fun and enjoying yourself is often enough to get you noticed. That awkward sitting around thing that women often do, hoping to catch someone's eye while they nurse their drinks in silence and desperation, is not going to lure him over. Be careful not to look like you're having too good a time, though – he might not feel comfortable enough to come over and break up the party.

Once you're relaxed and happy, give him a quick glance, catch his eye and then look away again. Try it again a few moments later – only this time, give him a half-smile too, to indicate that you wouldn't be averse to his coming over for a chat. If you're in a situation where you're close enough to hold eye contact, keep it going for a few seconds and smile. It's just about the best signal there is.

However, be aware that some men just won't come over. You might just need to go out there and be brave. If he's swapping signals, he may well be interested, just not quite brave enough to come over himself, especially if you're in a mixed-sex group where he can't be convinced – in spite of your signals – that he won't get set upon by your boyfriend!

BEING A NATURAL FLIRT

♥ Why does it seem so simple for some people to flirt with ease, while others get tongue-tied? It's generally down to confidence and feeling at ease with yourself. Some people find it easy to flirt in a business context, but become hopeless in a social one. The expression 'natural' doesn't exclude those who have had to learn to flirt rather than being blessed with flirting skills from an early age, but the following traits are generally found in people with an innate ability to flirt. However, many of these traits can be learnt and will develop with increased self-confidence and self-esteem.

Natural flirts have:

- Good self-esteem

- Belief in themselves

- The flexibility to develop a rapport with a wide range of people

- A positive and optimistic attitude to life

- A way of making people feel comfortable in their company

- An ability to ask questions and to listen properly

- Good instinct about what makes other people feel good

- An awareness of their own sexuality and its power

- The ability to pick up on other people's reactions

- A good sense of when to carry on to the next stage and when to stop flirting

- Fun!

Natural flirts enjoy:

- Meeting people

- New and different social occasions

- Using language to its full advantage

- A shared sense of humour

- Making and managing eye contact

- Giving compliments and making someone else feel good

LEARNING TO FLIRT

So much of learning to flirt is about developing the right attitude. It is *not* about what you wear, how you wear it or exactly what you say. Nor is it a loner's art. You can't learn to flirt unless you actually get out and meet and interact with people. You can try out your newly-acquired skills, one at a time, in a variety of different social situations. The essence of flirting is being able to radiate all the best bits of yourself, so that other people want to know more and are attracted to you. Accept that not everyone is going to like you and that you will get the odd knockback along the way. It happens to all of us. Just hold your head up high, and move on.

Flirting dos:

- First and foremost, you need to like yourself and learn to accept compliments with grace and without putting yourself down.

- Smile and pay people compliments. Tell that work colleague that her new haircut looks great, or tell someone how much you appreciate their advice if they've been helpful.

- Spend less time worrying about your past mistakes and more time thinking about the future. Take a look around you and see what's happening *now*. If your social life is stale and stagnated, do whatever it takes to improve the situation and look for new ways to meet people.

- Some of us are born worriers, introverts and pessimists. It's difficult to turn this around, but not impossible if you work at it over time. Try to be more optimistic and *don't* beat yourself up if you make mistakes, however impossibly huge they might seem at the time. We all do it and learning to flirt, just like any other skill, takes time and practice.

• Learn to modulate the tone, speed and pitch of your voice.

• Cultivate a sexy laugh – but make sure it doesn't sound too tinny or false: just something that you feel comfortable with.

Flirting don'ts:

• Don't dumb down or look miserable, bored or snooty.

• Don't flirt in packs – he may think all his Christmases have come at once if there's a group of cuties drooling over him, but flirting is essentially a one to one art-form, *not* a group activity.

• Don't invade someone's personal space – by all means lean in a little, but not so that they feel trapped!

• Don't be sarcastic or rude – it's not attractive!

• Don't go overboard when showing and using your body to its best advantage. A glimpse of cleavage is a whole lot more enticing than your D-cups running over.

• Don't stare unblinkingly when making eye contact – you'll just appear scary.

• Don't look over his shoulder when flirting with him – he will feel as if you're searching for your next victim.

• Don't ignore the signals – if he's not interested, let him go.

• Don't be too keen too fast. It's off-putting and seems desperate.

• Don't drink too much and ruin all that good work!

Sex

*S*ex – and preferably good, satisfying sex – is absolutely key in a relationship. There are few relationships that survive without sex, but even fewer where lack of full sexual contact is regarded as desirable by both parties. Initial attraction is *all* about sex – fancying someone, lust, chemistry, call it what you will – all roads lead back to sex pretty soon.

Sex is what we have with our lovers – rather than our friends – it bonds us together, giving us a level of intimacy beyond friendship, however close that may be. It's a form of stress release, immense pleasure, costs nothing, has no calories and research has shown that it both strengthens our immune system and lengthens our lives. Not a bad package of benefits! Added to that it makes us feel wanted, sexy, confident, cared for and relaxed. That's good sex, of course. Bad sex or sex that you have to persuade someone to have against their better judgement makes you feel frustrated, unattractive, unwanted, tense and dents your self-confidence big time. No one can have a great sex life all the time, but satisfying and fun sex is just so important in a relationship that it really is worth ensuring that you nurture it as much as possible.

THE NITTY-GRITTY

♥Dating and sex can be a minefield. When is the time right in a new relationship? My personal view would be after date two, three or four – when the excitement is still raw and the *frisson* is starting to build. If the chemistry's definitely there, he makes you laugh, the only appetite you've got is a sexual one and you're starting to trust him, the time could be right. But, it *is* entirely an individual choice. If you feel ready and comfortable on the first date, go for it (making sure you protect yourself!). If you want to wait a month or more, then do so. But I would sound two warnings from the bows.

Wait too long, and that gorgeous, attractive, seemingly patient man just might wander into an adjacent field where the grass is definitely more welcoming if not greener. When a man is not sleeping with a woman, he can often feel that he's not really in a relationship at all.

Conversely, if you jump into bed too willingly on the first date, that deeply unfair but perennial old chestnut comes into its own. While you are just going with the flow and doing what feels right, he just may (and if he doesn't then his mates probably will) think you're too easy and too willing. But of course he is just doing what comes naturally and what's expected of him. Most men wrestle with a constant dilemma. They'll wine and dine you, schmooze, flirt and do anything to get your knickers off on the first date, but while a huge part of their minds is urging you to say 'yes', another part is wanting you to say 'no' to show them that you are not simply an easy lay, or worse still a slapper, slag or whatever other choice words some men have for a woman who is also just doing what comes naturally. And definitely do *not* sleep with someone on the first date when you've had too much to drink – in fact keep that drinking level to fun rather than comatose. Guilt, regret and nausea are not what you should be feeling the following morning.

I have known men who, in spite of their initial, keen impressions of a woman, sleep with her on the first date, have great sex and then don't bother to call again and so she becomes that miserable state of affairs – the 'one-night-stand'. Men often want that impossible mixture – the purity of a virgin with the experience of a whore – and just find themselves unable to cope with the girl who says 'yes' too easily. One-night-stands can leave you feeling shabby, used and just baffled. It may be reassuring to know that it's unlikely to be your sexual performance that's at fault – some immature men are just programmed that way. Even in the 21st century, the one-night-stand is still predominantly a male domain, whether they began the night with that thought in mind or not. I certainly don't know too many women who go out with the intention of getting pissed, pulling and post-coitally dumping.

So don't feel pressurized, don't feel abnormal and do what feels right for *you*. Even if you're older, highly experienced and definitely no virgin, there are times when sex feels right and times when it doesn't. Never base your decision simply on your hopes for the future of a new relationship or on your fear of jeopardizing it early on.

THE 'GIB' FACTOR

♥ How do you know if he's got that 'GIB' factor? What is GIB? It's Good In Bed, of course! The following are not foolproof (if only…) but the odds are definitely in his favour if:

He dances well – if he's got rhythm on the dance floor then it's a pretty good bet that he's got rhythm in the sack. It's pretty obvious really – in order to dance well and sexily, he's got to have confidence and be in tune with his body: two pretty powerful ingredients in inspired sexual performance. If he's standing with his feet rooted to the floor while swaying his upper torso in some amorphous, unrelated-to-the-music rhythm or, alternatively, leaping around like a whirling dervish on speed, he's probably going to be a lacklustre lover. However, make sure that he's also making eye contact with you and that you're both interacting as you dance. The arrogant guy who dances in a swaggering, snake-like fashion may just turn out to be more selfish than hot in bed.

He has style – any man who knows what he looks good in has the bodily awareness that makes for a good lover. He doesn't need to be Armani man or spend a fortune on his clothes, but he needs to look sexy, well dressed and relaxed. He doesn't need to have bulging biceps or a six-pack, but he does need to give off a sense of style and clothes awareness. Rugby shirts can look cool, but football shirts rarely do (unless worn on the field by the likes of Beckham or Owen). Nothing beats a well-cut pair of jeans and a crisp linen shirt or a plain black or white short-sleeved T-shirt. Shirts can be in or out – depending on the physique.

He's adventurous with food and enjoys dining – it kind of follows that a guy who enjoys and savours his food and is willing to try something new at the dinner table is also willing to try something new in bed. It's all down to hedonism. If he seeks and takes pleasure from good food and drink, he's bound to be the same about sex. If his idea of a good meal is shovelling down a greasy kebab to soak up the beer on his way back from the pub, he may well just take the same approach in bed – a quick shag to fulfil his needs and he'll roll over and go to sleep…

His touch is generous and electric – being tactile is critical to the GIB factor. Too little and he'll come over as nervous, hesitant and uncomfortable. Too much too soon and he'll just seem too eager and intrusive and the whole event might just be over too quickly. Good signs are: if he stands so close to you that your bodies are almost touching; if he strokes your hand, lingering over each finger rather than just holding it limply; if your urge is to lean in and move closer, and your breathing quickens as desire begins to stir.

He's a great kisser – if he kisses you firmly and passionately and manages to caress you elsewhere at the same time, book the five-star with the four poster now! The best kiss is passionate and long (though not so long that you begin to wonder if you fed the cat before you came out), with variety. Nibbling, licking, biting, softly then firmly and back to gentle again, all indicate potential sexual variety. Multi-tasking is not really a male thing, but if a man can concentrate on two things at once in bed, then the pleasure zone awaits. Playing aggressive tonsil tennis with his tongue implies a possible lack of foreplay, with a '0–60 in five minutes' approach.

He knows what he wants – a confident man is really sexy. A man who has a clear idea of what gives him pleasure is often willing to do the same for you. Men like this usually know what clothes and hairstyle suits them, are fulfilled in their work, flirt well and make you feel good. Although he may not be the cutest or fittest guy in the room, a confident man will make you feel special in any situation. Add this to the ability to be funny and not take himself too seriously, and you've got a heady cocktail in the bedroom.

SEXUAL PERFORMANCE

♥ Worrying about sexual performance can become a self-fulfilling prophecy. The more we fret about how 'good' we are, the less likely we are to relax and 'perform' well. These words are inside quotes because performance is so subjective, and anyway, you're not there to pass a test. *None* of us are great in bed every time. Tiredness, stress or just not really being in the mood all affect our sexual performance. We also worry about being too good – does

Condoms

Is it acceptable for a woman to carry around a condom or two? Does this mean that she's a slapper, up and ready at a moment's notice for casual sex, or does it mean that she values her life far too much to risk an unpleasant sexual disease or even HIV and AIDS? Let's face it, it's always possible that we might have a little too much to drink and sleep with someone earlier than we might if we were sober, isn't it? Don't show your condoms off – just keep a couple in your handbag as you would keep a spare tampon or two even if your period's not due for days. Your period won't come on any faster just because you're carrying a tampon any more than you're more likely to leap into bed with the first available candidate just because there's a condom secreted at the bottom of your bag. It's too easy to think that a man will always have them at the ready, just because he's the one who has to wear one. I wouldn't want to play Russian Roulette with my life on that assumption, would you? Yes they're ugly, cumbersome and get in the way – so are life belts, but it would hardly be the objection when you were drowning, would it now?

that mean he might think we've done it too often before? Believe me, if you're a wildcat in the bedroom and he gets off on that, never beat yourself up about it. You're doing what comes naturally and having fun and there's no earthly, sensible reason why that should be related to the number of sexual partners you've had.

GREAT SEX THE FIRST TIME

♥ As we get to know someone better and become more intimate with them both physically and emotionally, our sex lives should definitely improve. However, first-time sex with a new partner needn't be a daunting, clumsy process any more than it should be the best sex we've ever had. There are some great plusses to first-time sex – it's raw, it's new, it zings with sheer lust and anticipation and can be fantastic with a little basic preparation. Without that preparation it can be awkward, all over too soon and frankly disappointing for both partners. Be aware of the following before you sleep with someone for the first time in any new relationship:

Be prepared – pick the right time and place. Set the mood by turning the lights down, lighting scented candles and playing a little atmospheric music. Nothing too slushy, but definitely no heavy metal either! And make sure you have some condoms to hand – literally. They are one of life's more tedious necessities and you don't want to be wondering just which drawer you've left them in at the crucial moment.

Don't unwrap all your presents at once – this is not a contest to see how many different sexual positions you can achieve in one night. You have nothing to prove. Just relax and have fun.

Don't expect fireworks – Sometimes it just takes a little time to find your equilibrium in bed. Just because the chemistry's there, it doesn't ensure that you'll have perfect sex the first time. You may not come or he may not be able to sustain an erection. You're both nervous – it happens. As long as you talk about it and laugh – not *at* each other, but *with* each other – one less-than-perfect sex session should not jeopardize the future of your relationship.

Relax and stop worrying – he's not judging your body. Well, he is a *little*, but if he's a decent guy he will gladly overlook most of your so-called 'faults'. If you really feel that they are that awful – and bodies vary hugely, so they're probably not – then warn him if it makes you feel more relaxed. It's unlikely that a few stretch marks, cellulite dimples or wobbly bits will put him off. He'll be fretting too – about his love handles, the size of his penis or premature ejaculation. Your concerns are nothing compared to his – trust me. There may be 100 things you know you like in bed, but let him try and find out for himself the first time. This is not the moment to tell him you like his fingers stroking your little toe or his tongue in your armpit. Kiss him slowly, stroke him gently, spend as much time as possible on foreplay without going headlong to the main event within the first few minutes. Take your time and enjoy…

NO STRINGS ATTACHED – CASUAL SEX

♥ The term 'casual' implies something relaxed and laid back, which at its finest – and with both parties in the same frame of mind – it can be. The trouble is that the term is also loaded with those male-imposed value judgement words 'slut', 'tart' and 'slapper', and can all too easily earn a girl that equally unpleasant term 'a reputation'. Although unspecified in its precise quality, it's rarely a good one…

If you're not searching for the perfect long-term mate – you may have just come out of a long-term relationship and be reluctant to go headlong into another – but you do miss sex, then here's the lowdown. While casual sex lacks depth and intimacy (the real reason for sex in a meaningful relationship), it certainly has some things to recommend it:

Casual sex – the plusses:

• You don't have to worry about what you feel for each other and you can indulge in the physical satisfaction only.

• You can feel totally uninhibited.

• You can carry out a sexual fantasy without worrying about being laughed at or rejected.

• You can choose a partner who excites you sexually but with whom you would be unlikely to be compatible in the long-term.

• It feels naughty and out of bounds, and therefore more exciting.

• It's lust, lust and more lust.

Casual sex – the minuses:

• Feeling guilty or cheap afterwards – if this is how you're feeling, then it may not be the way to go for you.

• *Always* keep, carry and insist on using condoms.

• Be careful how many people you tell about your affairs – you may feel totally at ease with yourself, but others may be quicker to judge. If you don't care what they think, then fine.

• Beware of married or attached men. You're playing with fire.

• Friends' husbands and boyfriends are *definitely* off limits. Seems obvious, I know, but mistakes can be made…

• Keep focused and try to keep your feelings under control. Sex is such an intimate activity, and great sex such a joy, that it can be easy to start falling for someone originally chosen as a casual partner. Don't risk a broken heart – either tell him (you never know, he may be beginning to feel the same way too, but don't bank on it), or get out of the situation while the going is good.

• Take extra care and don't take unnecessary risks. Don't go back to his place until you know him better. If you live on your own, make sure a mate knows where you are. Trust your instinct – if there's even a whiff of anything slightly dodgy about him, jettison him straight away.

Techno-Dating

We live and date in a fantastic age. While previous generations only had the traditional meeting places – parties, dances, through friends and so on – we have a whole range of new ways to meet people, some technology based, some just the brainchild of some creative person tapping into the huge potential of the ever-increasing singles market. A whole range of relatively new ways of communicating such as mobile phones, text messaging and email have radically altered the rules of dating over the last few years. While internet dating and text flirting may not be on the brink of taking over the world of dating completely, they are useful methods of meeting and keeping in contact with people and a great 'add-on' to the more conventional methods, giving you even more options to consider.

LOVE @ FIRST SITE – INTERNET DATING – THE BASICS:

♥ There are several million of us out there looking for love on the World Wide Web at any one time. However, websites vary enormously. Some are little more than 'meet markets' asking for the most basic of details, i.e. sex, age, job and location. Better sites probe further about factors such as your education, political affiliation or faith (if any), interest in the arts, sport and travel, favourite social activities – even your attitude to housework and the newspapers and magazines that you read. The more detailed the information given, the more likely you are to enable a microchip to match you up. Many of the internet dating sites are international, so unless you want to be contacted by people from all over the world, it's better to restrict your search to people living relatively close to your place of work or home.

For a smallish sum each month, you can tap into tens of thousands of possible partners. It's always better to post a photo on the site as this will result in a higher number of approaches or replies as well as making your virtual self seem more real. There are some seriously good-looking men out there (as well as some very sad cases indeed), but be warned – not all are what they seem. Some men post photos of themselves that are 10 years old or more or, worse still, simply not of them at all. What if they don't have a photo? Rather than hiding their light under a bushel, they're likely to be either horrendously ugly or married (and therefore living in fear of being recognized).

As with any other kind of dating, it's best to be honest from the outset. Your age, job, smoking and drinking habits, music tastes, sport and social interests and so on, should reflect the real you accurately. The only proviso here is that you should adopt a cyber 'handle' that isn't your real name, otherwise the handful of nutters out there will find you easily traceable when they add 2 + 2 to the rest of the information. Try and think of a fun name, too. MsPerfectnot or Sassychick is preferable to Jane123 or Nicegirlseeksbloke. Also, as well as making your profile as honest as possible, make it as much fun and as appealing as you can. There's a lot of cyber-competition out there!

You can check out the photos of literally thousands of men, depending on how broad your categories and preferences are – such as age, location, level of education, looks and so on. You can be proactive and mail promising candidates through the site when they're offline, or message them (often called whispering) when they're online, or you can just wait for someone to get in touch with you. If the messages are offensive in any way – and some have to be seen to be believed – many sites allow you to 'block' people so that they can't get back in touch with you again, but they won't know that they've been blocked by you.

You're under no obligation to answer any of your messages, of course, but if they're inoffensive enough, it's polite to reply even if they don't float your boat. Sometimes, though, even a knockback is enough to encourage further contact from some thick-skinned men. When you've taken a little time to find out about them and establish whether or not you share any common ground and humour, you could arrange to chat to them on the phone with a view to setting up a date. This is always a good idea as his voice and phone manner will tell you a lot about him. Some of the guys, while happy to chat online or nineteen to the dozen on the phone, balk at actually meeting you. Presumably, they have something to hide (such as a wife and four kids), are not what they purport to be or are just computer nerds getting off on a virtual conversation or two.

People often wonder how safe internet dating is. My view is that there are certainly crazy guys out there, but if you choose your website with care, exercise caution and use your instincts wisely, it's no more dangerous than meeting a stranger in a bar or a club.

Safe cyberdating:

• Don't choose a sexually provocative handle, unless you want a flood of dirty messages. MissWhiplash or Sexkittengivesgoodhead are not great options.

• Be wary of the handles than men give themselves – Pussylicker or Bondagemerchant are not likely to be happy to settle for a first date over a Starbucks café latté.

• Be very cautious about giving away your mobile phone number – wait until your instincts tell you that it's right.

• Take it slowly – don't ask for or accept a face-to-face date after just a few 'whispers'.

• Don't believe everything you read – use your instincts and judgement carefully.

• Block or report the offensive jerks – most websites dump 'em after a number of bad reports.

• Setting up a Hotmail account, or similar, without using your real name, is a good idea for emailing virtual strangers.

• Don't give a guy your business address unless you really feel you can trust him – you don't want him stalking your office.

• If you have his full name, check him out prior to the date on a good search engine such as Google, or check Friends Reunited.

- Always meet in a public place like a bar, pub or coffee shop.

- If you feel at all uncomfortable, threatened or compromised, excuse yourself and leave.

- Always let a girlfriend know where you are and ask her to ring your mobile an hour or so into the date.

- *Don't* get into his car unless you feel ultra-safe.

- *Don't* ask him back to your place on the first date.

- *Definitely* don't go back to his!

- Don't even think about falling in virtual lurve – you *must* meet him first.

PROS AND CONS OF CYBERDATING

♥Internet dating is definitely losing its stigma and becoming an increasingly acceptable way of meeting men – just mention it to a group of people and watch the other internet daters come out of the closet! Where else could you find such a wide and varied selection of men all looking to date?

Pros:

- It's a great hunting ground for busy, single professionals, especially if you work in a female-dominated industry.

- You can log on whenever it suits you – after work or a night out or over breakfast. There will always be people to chat to online.

- You can go on a virtual date and flirt to your heart's content, while wearing no make-up and your tattiest underwear.

- You can often find out more about someone before dating them than you could from a bar or club pick-up.

• Even if your dating doesn't work out, you can still chat or whisper when they're online – there's a bonding process in both of you being honest enough to say you're still looking for love.

• You can *always* have a date if you want one…

• It's essentially anonymous, so you can have as much fun as you like without fear of judgement.

• It's a fast way of meeting a lot of different men.

• If all your girlfriends are dating or settled and your social life needs a boost, it's a great way to meet people on your own.

• If you've just moved to a new area or hardly know anyone locally, it can help ease you into the social scene.

Cons:

• Men are often not what they seem (see pages 79 and 113).

• Some of the 'men' are actually women or groups of women having a laugh at your expense.

• Men's descriptions of themselves vary wildly – from the modest but gorgeous guy who describes himself as 'quite good-looking' to the (sadly) more common, overweight, boggle-eyed vision of horror who describes himself as 'athletic' and 'stunning'!

• It's an easy playground for married men looking for some extra-marital fun – some are honest about this, others not.

• You may get into a conversation with someone who seems divine, only to find out that they live hundreds of miles from you.

• Some men go from 0–60 in five 'whispers' – they start out in a friendly and chatty manner, then immediately progress to how they want to have you on the kitchen table.

♥ Some guys just can't type, so you'll have to put up with a lot of bizarre spellings. There's usually no spell check on internet dating sites.

♥ Some of the longer messages are clearly from cut 'n' paste merchants and are impersonal and often dull approaches.

♥ Guys might not actually want to meet you – preferring the anonymity, safety and fantasy of virtual dating to the real thing.

♥ There are a lot of women out there. Some men – especially the more attractive ones – go into a feeding frenzy of dates, so you are unlikely to be the only one that they are wooing/seeing.

♥ Some men are just after sex, whatever they might say – but hey, no change there then!

♥ There are some irritating and oft-repeated acronyms. LOL (laugh out loud) is one you'll see time and time again.

THE 21ˢᵀ-CENTURY DATING AGENCY
THE BASICS:

♥Dating agencies have come a long way since the days when it was a simple matter of filling out a Sunday supplement questionnaire, sending it off and lo, a mixed bag of male profiles was delivered to your door. They are now operating in a much more competitive world and have had to spruce up their act. Dating agencies – or introduction agencies as they now prefer to be called – tend to be for the more 'mature' client (30-plus) and have diversified into intimate dinner parties (and even lunch dates for busy office workers who find it hard to get away for an evening). They are not a cheap option, but rather than a microchip choosing your ideal guy, an experienced member of staff will analyze your profile to find you a suitable match. They also vet their clients, so you're far less likely to end up with the kind of weirdo that tends to trawl the web pages of internet dating sites, although some agencies also have allied – and vetted – websites of their own.

Pros:

- There's a human, hand-picked range of men to choose from.

- You can be as specific as you like about the kind of guy you want to meet.

- The men tend to have money – it's not a cheap option.

- They also tend to be serious about having a meaningful relationship, rather than just looking for sex.

Cons:

- Even the most skilled staff member can't legislate for chemistry – the stomach-churning hots that you get when you see someone gorgeous.

- There's no hiding your light under a bushel here – you have to be serious and focused about finding a mate.

- It's expensive and not guaranteed.

- It's somehow more calculated and clinical than other ways of meeting a guy – and not as suitable for more independent types who like to do the choosing.

PERSONAL ADS – THE BASICS

♥We've all seen them – those small ads in the back of the local rag or the nationals where a profile is squeezed into just a few words and some choice acronyms to get maximum value for money. GSOH (Good Sense of Humour) is a favourite, though it always looks like GOSH to me! (I always wonder who would 'fess up to a BSOH!) Trouble is, a lot of these ads have a bit of a reputation as a joke – it's believed that they're frequented by marrieds, fetishists and BDSM merchants. And yet I have at least two sets of friends – who are definitely *not* cross-dressing, sado-masochistic weirdos from Canvey Island – who have actually got married as a result of placing or responding to these small ads. So while some us may sneer at them, they clearly can work.

If you do consider placing an advert – or even replying to one – be wary of where you look. In a lot of local papers, the lonely hearts ads are squeezed in between sales of second-hand cots and second-hand cars, so these men come with no guarantees that they aren't soiled goods which fail all safety standards. On the plus side, you will often get a voicemail box, enabling you to judge someone's voice and humour before agreeing to meet them. Also, meeting a guy this way does avoid the cheesy chat-up line scenario of the local bar.

READING BETWEEN THE LINES

♥Apply the same rules that you would when reading estate agents' hyperbole, e.g. 'compact' or 'bijou' = 'no room to swing a cat' and 'potential for the DIY expert' = 'total wreck':

• **Professional** = got a job

• **Creative** = hasn't got a job

• **TLC (Tender Loving Care)** = mummy's boy

• **Romantic** = soppy

• **Gentle** = a wuss

• **Sensitive** = shy

• **Old-fashioned** = dull

• **Looks unimportant** = a virgin and desperate

• **ACA (All Calls Answered)** = single and desperate

• **LTR (Long-term relationship)** = never had a relationship that lasted beyond the weekend

- **Fun-loving** = looking for a shag

- **Sexy** = ditto

- **Passionate** = looking for a shag and lots of 'em

- **Nights in** = looking for a shag, but mean with it

- **Open-minded** = looking for a shag with leather bells and rubber whistles on top

- **Very Good Looking** = vain

- **Laid back** = wants you to do all the running

- **Easy-going** = ditto

- **Free-spirited** = does drugs

- **Spiritual** = wants to do drugs with you

- **Highly sociable** = drinks heavily

- **Well-built** = fat

- **Cuddly** = obese

- **Animal loving** = doesn't get out much

Oh... and the pros, cons and safety tips are very similar to those of internet dating (see pages 114–117).

DATING EVENTS

♥There has been a recent trend towards big organized dating events for singles of 25-plus. With more than 7 million singles in the UK alone, there's clearly a huge potential market. Since starting in London, these events are now spreading to other major cities throughout the UK and further afield. They are advertised in the local press and radio and a number are linked to websites where you can send messages to possible datees both before and after the main event. *Chemistry* is one of the pioneers in this field, and remains one of the leading dating event organizers.

Although they are not a cheap option, these events are a great night out for singles offering a wealth of attractions on the night. These might include a clubbing area, salsa dancing lessons, speed dating, fortune-telling, a chill-out room, an area for soundbite talks on subjects such as flirting and body language plus a representative from an Internet or conventional dating agency. Icebreaker games, text dating and a whole host of other matchmaking devices conspire to create an evening of fun and chaos with ample opportunity to meet the maximum number of people in the shortest possible time. With up to 1,500 singles per night, it is clearly a highly lucrative business for the organizers. The first drink is usually free – thereafter you have to pay over-inflated prices for refreshments – but the atmosphere is terrific and there's certainly no shortage of upwardly-mobile singles all looking for a date. It's a measure of just how far we've come in stigma-free singledom that one such recent event, billed as the 'Desperate and Dateless Ball', was chock-full of glamorous, good-looking and seemingly undesperate singles all looking for a good time.

SPEED DATING

♥ Speed dating was imported from the USA, where it's been a huge success. Based on the key ingredients for chemistry and attraction – voice, humour and looks – it works roughly like this:

• Anything from 10 to 30-plus women and men meet at an agreed location.

• You are paired off at tables for two and given approximately three minutes to chat and get to know each other.

• You are each given a card to keep track of the people you meet so you can decide whether you would like to see them again. Without this, it could be difficult to remember everyone!

• After three minutes a bell or a buzzer goes, or music is played, signalling that the guy has to move to the next table while another one comes to yours.

• You discreetly mark your card as to whether you'd like to see him again – he does this too, but it's harder for him, as he has to keep moving on.

• As well as a break or two – depending on how many people are gathered together – the three-minute process repeats until all couples have encountered each other.

• At the end of the evening, there's usually a chance to mingle.

• You then hand your card in and if two of you have both 'ticked' each other, email addresses will be swapped care of the organizers and further contact can be made.

Clinical? Yes, but it's a good shortcut to meeting people, and saves spending several tedious hours with someone on a date when you know from the first few minutes there's no chance that you fancy each other or that the relationship could take off. Looks, humour, character and voice are instrumental in knowing whether there's chemistry there, and while speed dating can't give any guarantees – any more than any other kind of 'arranged' dating – it's certainly a start. And if you sat down, took one look, listened for a moment and thought 'no way', it's a hell of a time-saver before you have to make your excuses and go home. It may not suit the shyer or more tongue-tied person, as the pressure is definitely on to meet and greet in a pretty short space of time. It's also definitely worth having a drink first, just to loosen up (but keep it to just the one!).

Speed dating tips

• Smile – always a great start and a good icebreaker.

• Welcome the guy to your table – even if he looks like the creature time forgot, it will make him feel at ease.

• Hold your head up and make eye contact. It shows openness and confidence.

• Try an unusual question. 'What would your best mate say if he knew you were here?' or 'What's a nice guy like you doing in a place like this?' might be corny, but a lot better than the 'Where do you live?' or 'What do you do for a living?' that he's heard several times already.

• Wear a little discreet scent. It'll help mellow the moment.

• Look smart and sassy, but avoid too much cleavage spillage. He's there to talk to *you*, not to your bosom.

Dating Websites

The Internet has a minefield of advice on all aspects of dating; some sites, of course, are better than others. Some of my personal favourites are:

Relationship Advice
www.handbag.com
www.ivillage.co.uk
www.ivillage.com
www.DrDating.com
www.flirtzone.com
www.thedatingdoctor.com
wwww.nomeancity.org

Internet Dating
www.Udate.com
www.DatingDirect.com
www.Match.com
www.Kiss.com
www.LoveandFriends.com

Dating Events
www.chemistryevent.com
www.thesinglesolution.com

Speed Dating
www.speeddater.co.uk
www.ukspeeddating.com

Introduction Agencies
www.sara-eden.co.uk
www.drawingdownthemoon.co.uk
www.onlylunch.co.uk
www.clubsirius.com

For the boys
These sites are designed for men, but they make revealing reading!

www.askmen.com
www.getgirls.com

Books on Dating

Never Kiss A Frog, Marilyn Anderson (New Holland, 2003)

Men Like Women Who Like Themselves, Steven Carter and Julia Sokol (Bantam Doubleday Dell, 1997)

Date...or Soul Mate?: How to Know if Someone is Worth Pursuing in Two Dates or Less, Neil Clark Warren (Thomas Nelson, 2002)

Fear Busting: A 10 Step Plan That Will Change Your Life, Pete Cohen (HarperCollins, 2003)

Hot Relationships: How to Have One, Tracy Cox (Corgi, 2000)

Hot Sex, Tracey Cox (Corgi, 1999)

Supersex, Tracey Cox (Dorling Kindersley, 2002)

Would Like to Meet... Tracey Cox, Jeremy Milnes and Jay Hunt (BBC Books, 2002)

Increasing Confidence, Philippa Davies (Dorling Kindersley, 2003)

Speed Dating: The Smarter, Faster Way to Lasting Love, Sue Deyo (HarperCollins, 2002)

The Little Book of Getting What you Want, John Gray (Vermillion, 2001)

Flirt Coach, Peta Haskell (HarperCollins, 2001)

The Little Book of Flirting, Peta Haskell (HarperCollins, 2002)

The Dating Game, Jo Hemmings (New Holland, 2003)

Should We Stay Together: The Compatibility Test, Jeffrey H. Larson (Jossey Bass Wiley, 2000)

Super Confidence: The Woman's Guide to Getting What You Want Out of Life, Gael Lindenfield (HarperCollins, 1989)

The Secrets of Sexual Body Language, Martin Lloyd-Elliott (Ulysses Press, 2001)

Body Language, Allan Pease (Sheldon Press, 1997)

Body Language Secrets: Read the Signals and Find Love, Wealth and Happiness, Susan Quilliam (HarperCollins, 1997)

Hex and the City: Sophisticated Spells for the Urban Girl, Lucy Summers (New Holland, 2003)

Sex Positions: Over 100 Truly Explosive Tips, Lisa Sussman (Carlton, 2001)

Bad Girl's Guide to Getting What you Want, Cameron Tuttle (Chronicle, 2000)

Index

Go Girl!

THE TINY PERFECT
DINOSAUR
BOOK THREE

Presenting Brachiosaurus

by John Acorn with ▨
Illustrated by Ely ▨

A Somerville House Bo

ANDREWS AND McMEEL
A Universal Press Syndicate Company
Kansas City

Contents

This Is Brachiosaurus

One of the biggest dinosaurs that ever lived was *Brachiosaurus* (BRAK-ee-o-SORE-us). It got its name, which means "arm reptile," because its front legs were much longer than its back legs. It was a peaceful dinosaur that ate plants and lived in herds.

3

Discovery of Brachiosaurus

Brachiosaurus was first discovered in Colorado. In 1900, a man named H. William Menke found some huge bones where the city of Grand Junction is today. The bones had turned to rock and were now fossils. Menke and his friends carefully dug them out of the ground.

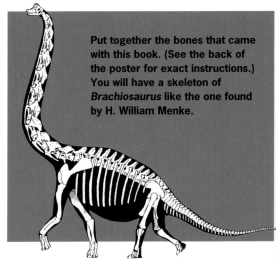

Put together the bones that came with this book. (See the back of the poster for exact instructions.) You will have a skeleton of *Brachiosaurus* like the one found by H. William Menke.

4

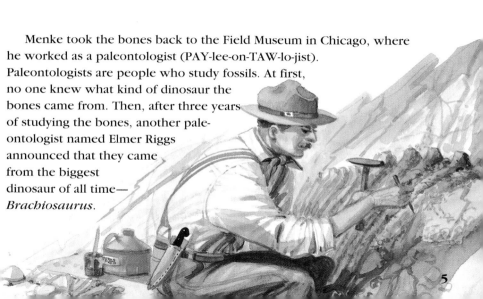

Menke took the bones back to the Field Museum in Chicago, where he worked as a paleontologist (PAY-lee-on-TAW-lo-jist). Paleontologists are people who study fossils. At first, no one knew what kind of dinosaur the bones came from. Then, after three years of studying the bones, another paleontologist named Elmer Riggs announced that they came from the biggest dinosaur of all time— *Brachiosaurus*.

The Biggest Land Animal Ever?

For a long time, paleontologists thought that *Brachiosaurus* was the biggest land animal that ever lived. After all, it stood forty feet (twelve meters) high. It was seventy-five feet (twenty-three meters) long, and it weighed about fifty-five tons (fifty-five tonnes). That's five times as much as the biggest elephants weigh.

Ultrasaurus

Brachiosaurus

Child

How could anything be bigger?

In 1979, an even bigger dinosaur was found in Colorado. The man who discovered it was James Jensen. He called the new dinosaur *Ultrasaurus* (UHL-tra-SORE-us). All he found was a shoulder blade and two back bones, but the shoulder blade was almost nine feet (three meters) long. That meant *Ultrasaurus* was twice as big as *Brachiosaurus*! Since the bones of *Ultrasaurus* and *Brachiosaurus* were the same shape, scientists think that these two dinosaurs were probably the same shape as well and that *Ultrasaurus* was just a bigger version of *Brachiosaurus*.

The biggest animal that ever lived on land or in the sea is the Blue Whale, which still lives in the oceans today. A big one can weigh 100 tons (90 tonnes).

If *Ultrasaurus* weighed twice as much as *Brachiosaurus*, it could have weighed 100 tons (90 tonnes) too.

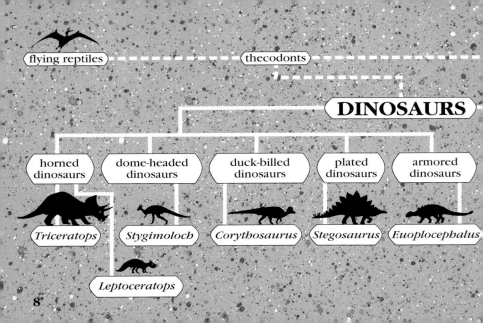

flying reptiles

thecodonts

DINOSAURS

horned dinosaurs

dome-headed dinosaurs

duck-billed dinosaurs

plated dinosaurs

armored dinosaurs

Triceratops

Stygimoloch

Corythosaurus

Stegosaurus

Euoplocephalus

Leptoceratops

8

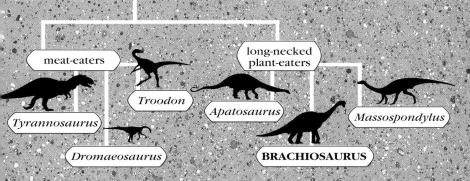

Family Tree

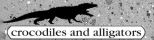

crocodiles and alligators

Paleontologists classify dinosaurs in many different groups. Here are some of the famous dinosaurs and the groups they belong in.

meat-eaters

long-necked plant-eaters

Troodon

Tyrannosaurus

Apatosaurus

Massospondylus

Dromaeosaurus

BRACHIOSAURUS

9

In Africa and Europe

What a surprise! In 1907, a German paleontologist found more *Brachiosaurus* fossils at a place called Tendaguru, in the country of Tanzania, in Africa. In fact, more skeletons of *Brachiosaurus* have been found at Tendaguru than anywhere else.

Then, in Portugal, more *Brachiosaurus* fossils were found. Portugal is a country in Europe. That means *Brachiosaurus* lived on three continents—North America, Africa, and Europe. (Continents are like giant islands that are surrounded by ocean water.)

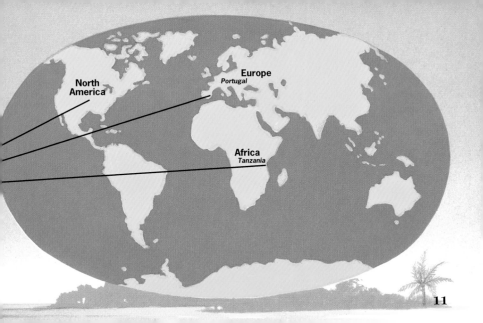

North
America

Europe
Portugal

Africa
Tanzania

11

The World of Brachiosaurus

The African *Brachiosaurus* fossils come from a bone bed. A bone bed is a place where the bones of many skeletons are found mixed up together. Most paleontologists think that bone beds were formed when a whole herd of dinosaurs died together.

Brachiosaurus fossils have never been found with the fossils of saltwater animals, so scientists think that *Brachiosaurus* never swam in the ocean. How could they get from North America to Africa and Europe without getting wet and salty? When *Brachiosaurus* was alive, the world was a very different place. All the continents that we know today were stuck

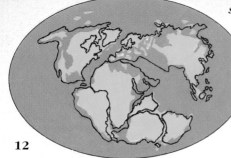

12

together. There were no oceans between them. *Brachiosaurus* didn't have to swim from one continent to the other. It just walked.

It was very warm then. Instead of summer and winter, there was a rainy season and a dry season.

There were lots of forests, but they were made up of evergreen trees and big ferns. *Brachiosaurus* lived in the forests, near lakes and rivers.

13

Brachiosaurus's Neighbors

Brachiosaurus lived with many other dinosaurs. In Colorado, there were meat-eaters like *Allosaurus* (AH-lo-SORE-us) and *Ceratosaurus* (serr-AT-o-SORE-us). There were long-necked plant-eaters too, such as *Diplodocus* (DIP-lode-O-kuss), *Apatosaurus* (ah-PAT-o-SORE-us), and *Barosaurus* (BARE-o-SORE-us). *Stegosaurus* (STEG-o-SORE-us), the plated dinosaur, lived there as well.

In Tendaguru, Africa, many of the same dinosaurs lived with *Brachiosaurus*.

Kentrosaurus

Barosaurus

Allosaurus was the most common meat-eater, and *Barosaurus* was the most common plant-eater. *Kentrosaurus* (KEN-tro-SORE-us) also lived at Tendaguru. It looked a lot like *Stegosaurus*.

Allosaurus

Ceratosaurus

Brachiosaurus

15

Like a Giant Elephant

If you look only at its body, *Brachiosaurus* looks a lot like an elephant. Even though it was huge, *Brachiosaurus*'s body was pretty slim from side to side. It wasn't round like a hippopotamus or flat like a lizard. If you look at the skeleton of *Brachiosaurus*, you'll see that its ribs pointed downward, not out to the sides.

Brachiosaurus's legs also pointed down. They were straight, like tree trunks, although they could bend at the knees for walking. The toes were short. All heavy animals today have this kind of leg, and scientists have invented a word for this build — "graviportal" (GRAHV-ee-PORT-all), which means built to carry heavy weight.

Today, all big heavy animals are gray or brown. Think about the elephant, the rhinoceros, and the hippopotamus. None of them have bright colors or patterns. *Brachiosaurus* probably had the same dull-colored skin.

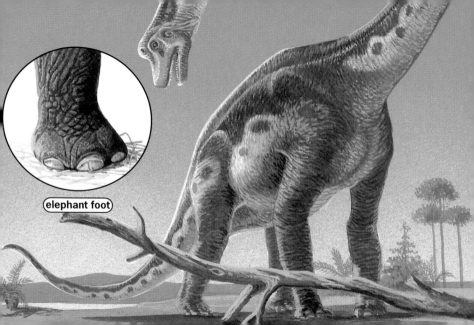

elephant foot

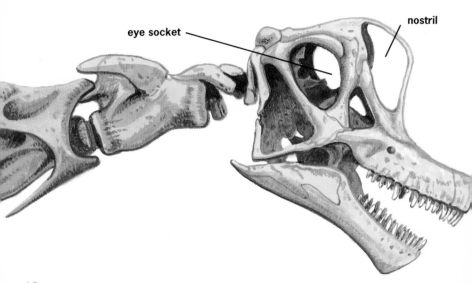

eye socket

nostril

A Tiny Head

Brachiosaurus's head was the same size as the head of a moose. It might look fine on a moose, but on a big animal like *Brachiosaurus*, the head looks very small.

The brain of *Brachiosaurus* was small too. It was only the size of a potato. Probably *Brachiosaurus* wasn't very smart.

Look at the skull. *Brachiosaurus* had big nostrils and big eye sockets. Most paleontologists think it could smell well and had good eyesight.

Brachiosaurus had spoon-shaped teeth for clipping plants but no molar teeth for chewing its food. Instead, it swallowed its food whole. Sometimes it also swallowed stones. Then, in a part of its guts called the gizzard, the stones ground up the plants. So *Brachiosaurus* did its chewing in its guts.

A Very Long Neck

The neck of *Brachiosaurus* was longer than its body. That makes paleontologists wonder how *Brachiosaurus* pumped enough blood up to its head. It must have had a very strong and large heart. One paleontologist decided that *Brachiosaurus*'s heart had to be the size of a grizzly bear. Other paleontologists thought that it was even bigger— the size of a three-ton (2.7 tonne) elephant! It must have been big, but maybe not *that* big.

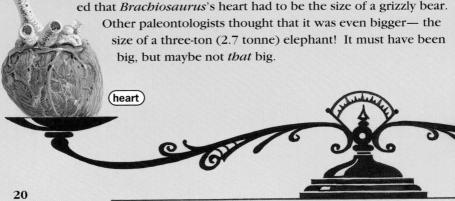

(heart)

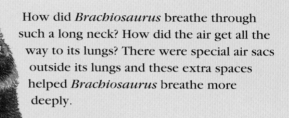

How did *Brachiosaurus* breathe through such a long neck? How did the air get all the way to its lungs? There were special air sacs outside its lungs and these extra spaces helped *Brachiosaurus* breathe more deeply.

grizzly bear

A Nose on Top of Its Head

Have another look at *Brachiosaurus*'s nostrils. Why were they so big? Why were they at the top of its head, instead of at the end of its nose? Scientists have four different answers for this question.

Good sense of smell?

One theory says that *Brachiosaurus* had a good sense of smell. You need a big nose for a good sense of smell, but a big nose on the end of *Brachiosaurus*'s snout would have got in the way. Perhaps that's the reason it was on top of its head instead.

A second theory says that *Brachiosaurus* used its big nose to make sounds and to call one another. Maybe the noise it made was the one you make when you blow your nose.

Communication tool?   **Elephant-like trunk?**   **Brain air-conditioning?**

A third theory says that *Brachiosaurus* had a trunk like an elephant's. Most paleontologists think this trunk would have looked funny, but many other animals with trunks also have big nostrils on the tops of their skulls.

Theory number four says that a big wet nose would have kept *Brachiosaurus*'s brain cool. When a brain gets too hot, it can't think very clearly.

23

A Dinosaur Giraffe

Of all the animals alive today, which one is most like *Brachiosaurus*?

Elephants look a bit like *Brachiosaurus*, but they have a big head on a short neck. *Brachiosaurus* had a small head on a long neck.

How about a giraffe? Giraffes are big animals with very long necks. Just like *Brachiosaurus*, they have small heads, and they eat leaves from the tops of trees. They use their long blue tongues instead of a trunk to grab leaves for food.

But a giraffe that was as big as *Brachiosaurus* would need thick legs to hold its heavy body. It would need bare skin, or it would get too hot. If it was dull-colored instead of spotted, it would look a lot like *Brachiosaurus*!

Of course, giraffes don't have a long, heavy tail. Neither do elephants. Both of them are mammals, but *Brachiosaurus* was a dinosaur. So really, there is no animal on earth today that is quite like *Brachiosaurus*.

In the Water or on Land?

When *Brachiosaurus* was first discovered, people thought it lived in the water. They painted pictures of *Brachiosaurus* standing on the bottom of a lake, with only its nostrils sticking out of the water. When it wanted to eat, they thought, it put its head down into the lake and chewed on water plants.

It turned out this idea was wrong. With the weight of so much water all around it, an underwater *Brachiosaurus* would not have been able to breathe!

Now, paleontologists think *Brachiosaurus* and its long-necked plant-eating

Ophthamosaurus

relatives were land animals. They walked on the ground, and they ate leaves from trees. How do we know that? There are fossil footprints that show where a group of them walked together on dry land.

Other fossil footprints show where one of these dinosaurs took a swim in a lake. Its toes made a strange set of footprints. It floated in the water and pushed itself along with its feet. *Brachiosaurus* could breathe when it floated on top of a lake, but not if it walked on the bottom of a lake.

Warm- or Cold-blooded?

Dinosaurs were reptiles. The reptiles that live today, such as crocodiles, lizards, and turtles, are all cold-blooded. That means that their body temperature is about the same as the air temperature around them. If it is cold outside, a cold-blooded animal will be cold too. Cold-blooded reptiles rest on their bellies and hold their legs out to the sides of their bodies.

Cryptoclidus

28

Archaeopteryx

Birds and mammals are warm-blooded. Even when it is cold, they can stay warm by making their own heat inside their bodies. Warm-blooded animals eat more than cold-blooded ones, and they are more active. They hold their legs underneath their body.

What about *Brachiosaurus*? It looks like a warm-blooded animal, since its legs were underneath its body. But it was too big to be warm-blooded. If it made its own heat, it would have become too hot. Paleontologists think it was something different. It wasn't cold-blooded, and it wasn't warm-blooded. Its body stayed warm just because it was so big. Every time it moved, its body would warm up. Food in its stomach made heat too. *Brachiosaurus* stayed nice and warm, even on chilly days.

An Early Extinction

The last dinosaurs died off and became extinct about 65 million years ago. They will never return. By the time the last dinosaurs died, *Brachiosaurus* had already been extinct for 85 million years.

Dinosaurs were on earth for 150 million years, but not all dinosaurs lived at the same time. Some became extinct early, and new ones evolved to take their place. *Brachiosaurus* lived at about the middle of the Age of Dinosaurs, in a time period called the Jurassic.

No one knows why *Brachiosaurus* became extinct. Maybe the climate changed, and *Brachiosaurus* was no longer able to live. Maybe some new kind of dinosaur ate all the baby *Brachiosauruses*. No one knows for sure. All we can do is guess.

young Brachiosauruses

31

Farewell to Brachiosaurus

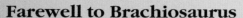

Brachiosaurus was a very special dinosaur. It was very heavy, it was very tall, and it was a plant-eater. Today, it is one of the most famous dinosaurs of all. As paleontologists keep on searching for clues from the Age of Dinosaurs, more fossils of *Brachiosaurus* will be discovered, and each fossil will tell us something new.

D1256436

ABRAHAM LINCOLN
AND THE SPIRITUAL LIFE

Abraham Lincoln
and the Spiritual Life

T. V. SMITH

Boston · THE BEACON PRESS · 1951

Printed in U.S.A.

Foreword

Pathos comes full where spirits narrow their vision to the level of geography. But sectarianism is a worse degradation than provincialism. Bodies are, of course, bound to regions, but spirits are not bound save as they bind themselves. To stumble over one's categories is, bound down to earth and time, to commit suicide on the install-ment plan.

These lessons are caught from example, however, more effectively than from pre-cept. Lincoln's life is better to this end than are all the books about him. Bound in many ways, himself Lincoln never bound. The skies of ideality were indeed the boundaries of his vision, the skies and nothing else. To the East he looked, to the West, to the North, to the South: he looked and saw and approached what others hardly dreamed was there. The record of his roomy discernment is a precious legacy for all mankind. What Lincoln saw, we too might see if we become more generous and if we were less afraid.

T. V. SMITH

Maxwell School
Syracuse University

ABRAHAM LINCOLN
AND THE SPIRITUAL LIFE

Three Secular Examples of Spirituality

Strange it may seem in a Christian culture that the purest American symbols of the uplifted life are citizens secular rather than religious in their outlook. This is not the most fortunate distinction to make among men — that between the secular and the sacerdotal — but since it is being more and more made, and made by sectarians to the detriment of their betters, it is fair to keep the record clear. Wise indeed it is as well as fair. For there is a lesson — yea, two lessons of spiritual import — to be learned from the testimony of our past.

The first lesson is negative: that one does not have to be "religious," as the word goes among churchmen, to contribute his share to the "spiritual life." The other lesson is positive: that if one be religious, he must at the same time be more than religious if he is to contribute his maximum to the high life of aspiration. What that "more" is that a religious man must have, we seek to let emerge without immediately obtruding it. Meantime, we may only remark that we do not exclude any form of religion as a path to spirituality and that we seek to grade down any form only as it seeks to rule out other means of spirituality, including other forms of religion.

Before turning now to certain high American illustrations of the independence of spirituality, and especially to Abraham Lincoln, let us say with eyes upon the past that the notion that religion has no monopoly upon the spiritual life is neither new insight nor radical. It is very old indeed, old and conservative. In the Christian tradition, it was Jesus who emphatically made a point of it. The best religious groups of his time he is reported to have compared to "whited sepulchers, which indeed appear beautiful outward, but are within full of dead men's bones, and of all uncleanness." So much for the deflation of any monopoly claimed by the religious. As for the more positive side, "the spirit bloweth where it listeth," without any finite weatherman, it would seem, to chart its course. Secularism is not opposed to religion. Secularism is opposed to sectarianism. High secularity is in favor of the whole of value, and is opposed only to what itself opposes some aspect of the life of the spirit. Neither our heroes nor we are opposed to religion. We applaud religious motivation, even when chary of religious intentions. We approve whatever religions unite in approving; we deny to any only what any denies to others.

It was at the hands of the intrenched religious indeed that Jesus was crucified, with full pathos into spiritual glory. Every age sees perpetrated, moreover, from the religion that has arisen around *his* name the same sadness—namely, that the spiritual suffer violence at the hands of the religious. The same lesson is written quite as large in Greek as in Hebrew ignominy. Socrates, the argumentative agent of the spiritual life in old Athens, had to down the cup blessed for his demise by the orthodox of the day. *They* said that *he* was an atheist! But let us look swiftly now at three American examples of high secularity before concentrating upon Lincoln as the mighty middle one.

Thomas Jefferson was never a church member, nor could he have been, churches being what they were in his day. It was not that he did not prize them; it was that, in a sense made curious by them, he prized churches and even religions too much: he prized them indiscriminately. "In all religions we see good men," said he simply and generously, "and as many in one as in another." He took them all in, whereas they shut one another out. "If I could not go to heaven but with a party, I would not go there at all." And of Calvinism, a popular form of Protestantism in his day, Jefferson was forced to conclude from the inhumanity of its god, that Calvin was worse than an atheist. "It would be more pardonable," in Jefferson's own words, "to believe in no God at all than to blaspheme him by the atrocious attributes of Calvin." How indeed could Jefferson have been formally religious when religious men all around him were worshiping a deity not even as good as they were? Yet it was this Jefferson, a secularist, who dignified man to the level of universal citizenship, with equal rights for all, who wrote the Declaration of Independence, who established religious liberty in Virginia (against the opposition of the religious!), and who later moved on a national scale to rob pious power of its poison by "erecting a wall of separation between church and state." It was this Jefferson who said: "I have no fear, but that the result of our experiment will be, that men may be trusted to govern themselves without a master. Could the contrary to this be proved, I should conclude, either that there is no God, or that he is malevolent." And, climaxing all this, a saying now engraved in marble above his heroic statue in Washington: "I have sworn upon the altar of God, eternal hostility against every form of tyranny over the mind of man."

Towering with Jefferson is one also high in spirituality, perhaps the highest of all Americans born to be woman. "Jane Addams," declared John Burns, the Englishman, "was the only saint America has produced." If she was formally religious, as barely she was,[1] this profession bulks small against the pure light of spirituality which was far in excess of anything formal. When she came to graduate from Rockford "Seminary," she refused to accept the certificate as long as Rockford was the sectarian place she had known and had rebelled against. And this refusal she persisted in until the mountain came to the adolescent! While at the school, she registered a free woman's disdain for the religion of her

---

[1] "But," writes her beloved nephew and official biographer, James Weber Linn, "her position did not at all please the priests, ministers and editors of religious papers of the community. Many of them assailed Hull House frequently during the first ten years of its existence, for its lack of specific religious activity." (*Jane Addams*, p. 204.)

dean, a typical devotee of whom the school-girl wrote: "She does everything for the love of God alone, and I do not like that." Though later, much later, Miss Addams joined a church for practical reasons, she could declare: "Christ doesn't help me in the least . . . he doesn't bring me any nearer the *Deity*. . . . My creed is low, *be sincere and don't fuss.*"

Born for the universe, this founder in Chicago of a "Cathedral of Compassion" could not narrow her mind and to any provincialism give up what was meant for mankind. It was from this sharp critic of the formal, including formal religion, that we have, nevertheless, that largesse of spirit, Hull House, and the magnificent mission that animated her whole life: "The modern world is developing an almost mystic sense of the continuity and interdependence of mankind — how can we make *this* consciousness the unique contribution of our time to the small handful of incentives which *really* motivate human conduct?" (Italics mine.)

Coming in time between that masculine seer of the spiritual life, dispensing his rays from Monticello, and this feminine pilgrim, radiating magnanimity from Halsted Street, there appeared at a historic moment, to stand immortally on the highroad of history, the sad-faced man from Salem, Illinois. Born in a log cabin of Kentucky, buried as a martyr from the White Mansion of the nation, Abraham Lincoln died as he lived, a secular mind clairvoyant of all spirituality. He did not join a church, nor could he have joined one, churches being what they were and his sense of fitness being what it was. He is reported to have said that he would join a church, if ever he found one roomy enough of spirit. Such was not to be found in the Christendom of his age. Jefferson was proud to be free; Lincoln was wistful. "Oh, why should the spirit of mortal be proud," as ran Lincoln's favorite poem. Unquestionably this wistful pilgrim of the spiritual often pined for some tenement of corporate clay to ease the austerity of the holy heights which he often climbed. But

he was too sensitive and too scrupulous
to claim as possessed what he did not even
comprehend. He saw and grieved over the
universal lot, bearing his piety in silence,
or conning it over in popular verse:

> The saint who enjoyed the communion of
> heaven,
> The sinner who dared to remain un-
> forgiven,
> The wise and the foolish, the guilty and
> just,
> Have quietly mingled their bones in the
> dust. . . .
>
> 'Tis the wink of an eye; 'tis the draught of
> a breath
> From the blossom of health to the pale-
> ness of death;
> From the gilded saloon to the bier and
> the shroud —
> Oh, why should the spirit of mortal be
> proud?

The negative lesson is now clear, nor
need we further emphasize it since our in-
tent is wholly positive. The part is smaller
than the whole, and fixation upon the part
may involve — alas, does usually involve —

some betrayal of the whole. But it is the whole to which the lesson points, leaving the parts such integrity as partiality can command. The spiritual life is, no less and no more, the *life of the spirit*. It is presumptuous to put material bounds to the spiritual. Any bounds inherited can but challenge aspiration to overpass them. In blowing where it listeth, the spirit blows conceptually as well as concretely. The categories of philosophy are but efforts to capture the spirit, that in captivity it may be turned to larger mission. The ideals of common life, no less than the concepts of philosophy, furnish universal techniques for its appropriation. Among the oldest and noblest of these ideal containers, both philosophical and popular, let us single out that trinity of value known as Goodness, Truth, and Beauty. From Socrates to the present, the mind of Western Man has sought to catch in these triune buckets the rich precipitates of spirituality.

Finitude prescribes partiality. Modesty prevails in the life of the spirit, lest secular servants of the spiritual stray with sacerdotal saints into the sectarian claim that one ideal — holiness, for example — is all there is of ideality. Specialization, in virtue no less than in virtuosity, is the secular incarnation of modesty. But what is necessary as crutches for the crippled can become crippling for the well. It is honorable if any man become a dependable agent of Goodness, or Truth, or Beauty. But we reserve our final honor for those who discharge their finite duties in the amplitude of the infinite. Such a saint — a Secular Saint! — was Abraham Lincoln.

Lincoln as a Moralist, Serving Goodness

A man, however saintly, is most fairly to be judged by his specialty. Few men can be known beyond that; for it is given to few men in modern times to have energy enough left over from the practice of specialized skill to distinguish themselves in general. It is enough for merit that one be a good doctor, a good lawyer, a good farmer, or a good mechanic. No excuse is adequate to constitute a proper reason for a man's not accepting his chief credit from what he claims best to do. Lucky indeed is the man, and fortunate his time and place, if he does superbly well his own work; unearned is the increment of virtue which comes from beyond the duty of specialized endeavor.

Leaving that larger guerdon for the moment, in Lincoln's case the smaller work to which he set himself was well done. He never became a distinguished lawyer, though he did well enough at the bar, considering his meager preparation and the pioneer opportunities. Anyhow, it was not law to which he apprenticed himself — not law, but politics. Law was the means. A man is to be finally judged in terms of the end which he chooses.

Let us see how well Lincoln discharged his main vocation, that of politics. Nobody denies the consummate art whereby Lincoln rose to final political place upon a stairway of only partial successes. Success is best to be judged in his case by the use he made of failures. Lincoln failed once of the state legislature; he failed once and for all of the U. S. Senate. He was elected once to the national House of Representatives but did not stand again — perhaps wisely did not dare to stand again. His four terms in the lower house of the General Assembly of Illinois, and his single term in the Congress of the United

States, were undistinguished, though not unsuccessful in terms of the end. Men come to honor by serving great ends greatly; men succeed through the mastery of necessary means. Through his undistinguished years, Lincoln was learning not only to use but also to dignify the means which politics is.

Democracy is not primarily a goal or any cluster of goals; democracy is a *going*. Rather than a way of arriving somewhere, it is a way of getting along, and getting along together. This method of living together is the give-and-take, the live-and-let-live, out of which do not normally come great things, but which is itself a very great thing. It was how to do this, and the coming to feel that the doing of it was indeed the greatest thing in the world — it was this double assignment to which Lincoln's apprenticeship in politics was devoted. Nor has many an apprenticeship been better spent.

Lest there be those who would misunderstand, let us state even more plainly what we are talking about. Lincoln was a politician, a politician more of the mine-run variety than of the extraordinary type. Politicians, too, are servants of the ideal, of the Ideal of Goodness, in the value trilogy which we have taken for our orientation. But the form of Goodness which politicians mostly serve is the interpersonal type known as Justice. Now Justice means many things, but in a democratic society it means above all one thing: it means a proportionate sharing of burdens but with a fair chance at benefits. In a democratic society men are encouraged to get ahead, and are allowed to get ahead as far and as fast as it can be done without inflicting undue burdens upon others as a result.

The distinguishing thing about politics as a struggle for justice is that wherever men differ about justice concretely — as mostly they do — all of them are initially to be regarded as in the right. Men, that is, have a right not only to their interests but to their opinions: to harbor them, to express them and to make them prevail as far as is permitted by a proportionate acceptance of burdens. But to say this of all men, that every man is right, is also to say that nobody can be allowed to monopolize the Right, or to get all that he thinks is right to get. That would be to render his "right" exclusive, and that is an honor unearned by any single right. That, simply, is the difference between democratic and totalitarian justice. The latter concentrates the power; the former distributes the power and the "right" which sustains it. There arises, then, as a democratic result of all men's being assumed to be in the right, the necessity of consent and concession, or as we simply say, of compromise. The abstract meaning of Justice must be kept vague, or at least ambiguous, so that its different concrete meanings may be legitimatized. Each man must find operative as benefits something of the meaning which he attaches to the ideal.

It was this method of composition, this art of compromise, that Lincoln learned — learned not only to use but also to honor. He learned, that is, not only how to make compromise succeed in practice, but how to make it appear for what it is, the very strategy of goodness. The harm that bad men do is hardly a circumstance to the harm that good men do, men who insist on being good in a manner that is monopolistic. The final form of goodness is that which keeps such monopolistic claims from cancelling out all goodness, the Whole destroyed by the jealousy of the parts. He who can persuade narrow-visored idealists to take less than they intended, in order to keep alive and fruitful the integrity of intention, is a secular saint in the field of Goodness.

Lincoln's apprenticeship to the art of compromise began when he joined eight other six-foot men, the "Long Nine," to get the capital of Illinois moved from Vandalia, where Lincoln *didn't* live, to Springfield, where he did live and was to practice law! He served himself well in that deal, but he served the state also in getting its capital nearer its geographical and populational center. He served the nation greatly, in a later event, through the *type* of compromise which he proposed with reference to slavery. But he served more magnificently in getting clear the very theory of compromise as the *modus operandi* of public morality and in recommending it as the collective reliance of civilized men in all generations.

Let us attend to this larger matter first, and then return to observe how fine Lincoln's sense was in choosing his distinctive compromise on the slavery issue. There are compromises *and* compromises in the human venture. When that is fully understood, the charge of his abolitionist contemporaries will not hold, not in the tone of voice which they used: the charge that he was a "middleman between a very modest right and the most arrogant and exacting wrong."

In arguing throughout a great speech — at Peoria, in 1854 — for the restoration of the Missouri Compromise, Lincoln made his main point, as later he immortalized it to Horace Greeley, not whether slavery were or were not to be established in Nebraska. What troubled him, as he said, was that "the spirit of compromise," as he well called it, would otherwise be "repudi-

ated" or "discarded, . . . from the councils
of the nation." It was this *"spirit of compromise,"* [2] as he continues, "which first gave us
the Constitution, and which has thrice
saved the Union." So much on the side of
fear. This on the side of hope: "We thereby restore the national faith, the national
confidence, the national feeling of brotherhood. We thereby reinstate the spirit of
concession and compromise, that spirit
which has never failed us in past perils,
and which may be safely trusted for all
the future."

The conventional moralist, in narrow
mood, if he napped a moment in that reading, might think that Lincoln had been
talking about the Holy Ghost — so per-
fervid are the goods which he attributes to
the success, so terrible the evils he credits
to the failure, of this lowly principle of
compromise. Indeed it is not irreverent
thus to describe what Lincoln was talking
about, though the sectarian mind will never
have it so. Concession *is* the holy spirit
of men who are determined to make a go

----

[2] Italics mine.

of their co-operation in spite of any and all differences. Lincoln saw as few men of sentiment ever see, how sticky is the notion of "brotherhood" (the term is his) unless it be between equals; and he saw more, that the only way to keep it between equals is to deny to anyone's conviction a priority of access to moral certainty. Liquidation — the eternal temptation of such priority — did not appeal to Lincoln, not even when done in the brotherly name of loving-kindness.

Brothers must be allowed to differ, and all men have to learn how to contain their differences over first things. Even in the sequence of war, one must eventually live at peace with those whom he has fought, and so he must do late with less resources what he might have done early with more. So Lincoln on Southern sectionalism in his First Inaugural: "Suppose you go to war, you cannot fight always, and when, after much loss on both sides, and no gain on either, you cease fighting, the identical old questions as to terms of intercourse are again upon you." That is bedrock thinking. The only art there is to sustain peace is already present as the political art of compromise. Here, then, is the very life blood of Justice. Goodness in general is self-annihilative if men of different convictions cannot come together by each yielding enough so that the other will not have to give all. The only way to save the soul of Justice is to save the faces of men who are diversely just.

The theory of this will be further understood through its practice at the hands of Lincoln, for Lincoln was its chronic practitioner. Those who try to distinguish him from Stephen Douglas by making Lincoln a man of principle in a sense that Douglas was not, have not understood the moral source of Lincoln's greatness. Lincoln knew no other way to preserve a Union that had been created by compromise than through its continuous practice, and he never thought beyond this category. Indeed there is no way of thinking beyond this category unless one is to transcend democracy itself. But there are many ways of thinking within the category.

Lincoln differed from Douglas in that he had a *better* compromise. It was better in that it was responsive to more factors — in a longer time-span. Douglas was willing to let slavery try to extend itself in the thought that God would cancel the effort; that is, that climate and other natural factors would foredoom slavery to failure, in spite of every Southern effort to extend it. But if God failed, then man too failed, and of all men those failed most who were weak and so least able to afford failure. If man succeeded, God would succeed; if God failed, man would have foreclosed his last chance to succeed. Piety to the past means acceptance of the past, since the past cannot be changed. Piety toward the future, however, means acceptance of responsibility to make the future the way we want it, while the chance is still ours. Lincoln's compromise — to leave slavery unmolested where it was, even to return fugitive slaves; but to forbid the spread of slavery where it was not — was a compromise that would have honored the future with hope for the mitigation of an evil which had to be accepted as inherited from the past. Such moral prowess yields statesmanship in content, as we have already seen it to constitute statesmanship in form.

Lincoln was, then, as good a politician as he knew how, and his skill exceeded all other men of his generation, if indeed it is exceeded by any men of any generation. But his distinguishing greatness is that he understood the law of progress, that in interpersonal and especially in intergroup relations, the higher the ideal the weaker, and the lower the ideal the stronger. The ideal of compromise is not high, not nearly as high as was then the ideal of abolition, but it is strong. Lincoln saw in the art of compromise itself the transforming genius whereby a low ideal saves a thousand lower values and gives room for a thousand higher values to flourish in groups smaller than the state, which meantime maintains order for all their efforts. Lincoln was a specialist in the field of Goodness, and as such was in his modest finitude a mighty agent of the spiritual life.

But he was an agent of the spiritual life conceived as servitude to Truth hardly less than of the spiritual life conceived as devotion to Goodness.

Had Lincoln been a busybody in other preserves of values while neglecting his own specialty, he might have anticipated the Russian Lysenko in charlatanry. But Lincoln was not meddling in a field outside his own domain of politics. He had no scientific training, and of course made no pretensions to science. He pretended to be what alone he was, a politician. It was in being what he was that there glinted forth, unintendedly and frequently unconsciously, reflections of light upon his own specialized virtue from the sun of the whole of man's spiritual empire.

Lincoln as Scientific in Spirit, Serving Truth

For a man to observe beyond the laboratory the attitude of scrupulosity which characterizes the scientist in the laboratory, is for him to go beyond the call of duty imposed by whatever specialization his own vocation enshrines. Lincoln was a lawyer; vocationally a lawyer, and a politician. This specialization in value commits its representatives to Justice, as that particular form of Goodness which is by nature interpersonal and intergroup. It is too much to expect of the average politician that he shall exemplify other canons of public endeavor than those which commend themselves to him as direct means to his own ideal end, to justice. The level of scientific scrupulosity is not high among politicians. So with most politicians most of the time, and so with all politicians some of the time.

But with Lincoln little of the time. His avocation as a spirit overshadowed his vocation as a mere man, and informed his practice through and through with the spirit of the whole. Lincoln trenched less upon the downright untruthful than most politicians, largely because he saw further than most: he saw around the corner and was informed of present circumspection by foreseen consequences. Instead of saying, as is easy and natural for a politician on the stump: "If you elect me, I'm your man; I'll do whatever you wish me to do," Lincoln said (in announcing himself the second time as candidate for the Illinois legislature):

> I shall be governed by [your] will on all subjects upon which I have the means of knowing what [your] will is; and upon all others, I shall do what my own judgment teaches me will best advance [your] interests.

The obfuscation of that statement but honors the ambiguity which is intrinsic to politics. Lincoln put it, however, in such fashion as at the same time to represent the maximum of truth which politics permits. The unclarity is necessitated by the fact that no representative, not even in our own poll-conscious days, ever knows with certainty what the majority of his constituents wants. He never hears at any given time from more than a small minority, not even in the heaviest mail; nor ever hears the certain tramp of the majority, not even when he puts both ears to the ground.

Lincoln's usual manner of keeping distance from the untruthful was to indulge in stories (not unlike the parables of holy men) which could mean different things to different hearers. Ambiguity is necessary for persuasion among free men who are equal, since not all men have the same prepossessions or are thinking the same things. Parables transfer the responsibility from the teller of the story to the hearers, achieving ingratiation without committing prevarication.

Consider this example, an example reported by Titian J. Coffey, in the New York *Daily Tribune:*

"I attended an old field school in Indiana," said Lincoln, "where our only reading book was the Bible. One day we were standing up reading the account of the three Hebrew children in the fiery furnace. A little tow-headed fellow who stood beside me had the verse with the unpronounceable names; he mangled up Shadrach and Meshach woefully and finally went all to pieces on Abednego. Smarting under the blows that in accordance with the old-time custom promptly followed his delinquency, the little fellow sobbed aloud. The reading, however, went round, each boy in the class reading his verse in turn. The sobbing at length ceased, and the tow-headed boy gazed intently upon the verse ahead. Suddenly he gave a pitiful yell, at which the school-master demanded: 'What is the matter with you now?'

"'Look there,' said the boy, pointing to the next verse; 'there comes them same darn three fellers again!'"

And looking out the window, where Lincoln had been looking, the visitor to whom the innocent story had been told saw coming to torment Lincoln once more the three Horsemen of Emancipation: Sumner and Wilson and Stevens!

Lincoln's stories often achieved amiability through ambivalence. But his respect for the truth was far more than strategic. The scientist is one who has learned to keep his mind open until the evidence is in, and then to follow the evidence in his conclusion. Disciplined by doubt, he is enabled to contain his hopes and fears, accommodating both to objective demands. There is something singularly hygienic in wanting the facts, accepting the facts, containing the facts, and then accommodating hopes to the factual. Such scrupulosity is not the usual human response. Quite to the contrary, man is a believing animal. He believes what is plausible. He believes what is convenient. He believes what is popular. He believes in short what is comfortable — and facts are rationalized into conformity. Most men illustrate in humble things what the professor of theology at Padua professed to Galileo: that there was no use of looking through the telescope because he already knew the new planet was not there! Had he not read the Bible and Aristotle backwards and forwards, and found nothing of it in either? So even if he looked and saw it, it would not be so; it would be a temptation of the devil to wean his soul from certitude! That is man; and not only religious man, though the servitude of credulity in religion is nowhere else surpassed.

In politics, however, it is at time closely approached. So much so that it is not humane that politicians in their sincere quest for justice be held responsible also for truth. When a politician is found who can and does carry into the specialization marked by Goodness the scrupulosity required by Truth, a luminary of unearned spirituality has swum into ken. Such a luminary was Lincoln.

Consider, by way of illustration, two remarks of his as we move toward more substantial exemplifications of this scientific spirit in the politician. Lincoln's general attitude is well represented in his introduction to his Springfield speech, accepting nomination to the United States Senate: "If we could first know where we are and whither we are tending, we could better judge what to do and how to do it." Predisposed always to an empirical orientation, he could later in the presidency summarize his procedure with reference to slavery by saying, "I claim not to have controlled events, but confess plainly that events have controlled me." Confirming this scientific predisposition, Lincoln's close friend Leonard Swett declared that "the whole world to him was a question of cause and effect — his tactics were to get himself in the right place and remain there still, until events would find him in that place." And Herndon quotes Lincoln's wife as reporting what Herndon confirms: that Lincoln's "only philosophy was, what is to be will be, and no prayers of ours can reverse the decree." Here is betokened a reliance upon causal laws, even in politics, which is worthy of a man of science.

This attitude deserves illustration now in the most crucial settings of Lincoln's life. Consider the point as dramatized in his dissertation on God's will. Providence is to the religious a presupposition. The scrupulous mind would, however, have to consult the complexion of events in determining the reliability of what is called providence, as of all claims. Wherever gods have been, devils also have been; and where both are, they sometimes get confused. When the religious cautioned Lincoln, the war leader, that more reliance should be put on prayer, Lincoln's reply was that "the rebel soldiers are praying with a great deal more earnestness, I fear, than our own troops." Generalizing this caution, Lincoln put his larger thought in these sentences of scrupulous dubiety:

The will of God prevails. In great contests each party claims to act in accordance with the will of God. Both may be, and one must be, wrong. God cannot be for and against the same thing at the same time. In the present civil war it is quite possible that God's purpose is something different from the purpose of either party. . . . By his mere power on the minds of the now contestants, he could have either saved or destroyed the Union without a human contest. Yet the contest began. And, having begun, he could give the final victory to either side any day. Yet the contest proceeds.

What conclusion does Lincoln come to in his soliloquy of dark pathos? None, none for certain; and that is the significant thing. A sloppy mind could have done more. A flabby mind could have done most, aligning Providence all on his own side. Such "noble impartiality of self-preference" is a thing as natural as it is cheap. Lincoln had a scrupulous mind, and a scrupulous mind will not on evidential matters conclude against the evidence, nor beyond the evidence, nor outside the evidence. The evidence for a unitary and decisive Providence is always ambiguous, rendered so by the simple fact that equally good men, yea, equally religious men, are on different sides of every important issue.

"You should not carry that pistol in your saddle-bag," called to him the wife of a Calvinist missionary of Lincoln's time and region. "You know, according to the Scriptures, that even if you met an Indian, he could not get you unless 'your time had come!'"

"But, yes," replied the perturbed preacher, "but suppose I met an Indian *whose time had come!*"

If there be a Providence, the most anybody can safely conclude about it is that nobody knows for certain what it is. And this is precisely the conclusion to which Lincoln came. As Stephen Vincent Benét so beautifully puts it:

All of them are sure they know God's will.
I am the only man who does not know it.

Nobody knows enough dogmatically to deny the possibility of Providence; nobody knows enough, on the other hand, to demonstrate its *ex parte* nature. This latter type of faith was, as the classic-minded may recall, precisely the kind of divine favoritism which Plato proposed in his *Laws* — moral atheism, he regards it — to treat with extreme rigor, in short, with death. But Plato was a totalitarian. In a free society it is punishment enough of credulity for the scrupulous simply to avoid association with such moral lassitude in the intellectual field. This on the negative side; but on the positive side, we must say more. For men who achieve scrupulosity under the buttresses of science, supported as they are by specialization and strengthened in morale by association with the like-minded, we save high honor. Even higher honor Mankind may justly bestow upon those who, in fields logically slipshod, as is politics, illustrate, nevertheless, a chastity of mind which such austerity toward credulousness reveals.

Lincoln climaxed such intellectual scrupulosity with a practice equally chaste. To the White House came, in 1862, a deputation of Christian ministers who had somehow discovered — so they said — what God willed Lincoln to do with reference to emancipation. "I am approached," began

[37]

he to them in a mood embarrassingly empirical, "with the most opposite opinions
and advice, and that by religious men who
are equally certain that they represent the
divine will." He hazarded then the opinion, hoping it would not strike them as
"irreverent," that if God was going to reveal to anybody what Lincoln's duty was,
He would reveal it to Lincoln himself. And
then he earns the accolade "scientific" by
adding:

> These are not, however, the days of
> miracles, and I suppose it will be granted
> that I am not to expect a direct revela-
> tion. I must study the plain physical facts
> of the case, ascertain what is possible,
> and learn what appears to be wise and
> right.

Obviously, for a scrupulous mind there
is no other recourse. The mastery of facts,
the study of moral appearances, and the
predication of conduct upon the background of facts and the foreground of what
is possible out of all that appears good —
this is the prompting of science in fields not

themselves as yet subjected to scientific techniques.

There is another large area, too, in which Lincoln demonstrates with equal cogency the scientific complexion of his mind. That is in his chronic distinction between what we have already called *certitude* and what the generality of men call "certainty." Now, certitude is what one is privately assured of but cannot publicly demonstrate. The difference between the evidence accepted by the credulous and that required by the scrupulous is colossal. W. K. Clifford has dramatized that difference, on the rigorous side, in declaring that "it is wrong always, everywhere and for everyone, to believe anything upon insufficient evidence." But what constitutes "sufficiency" for the scrupulous? It must be at least enough evidence to convince not only one himself, not only his friends who are already like-minded, but also his enemies in the general field of joint competence. Not until one can "exhaust the alternative hypotheses," as Pasteur in defense of science succinctly puts it, has he earned the right to announce as the truth any of his beliefs, however much certitude he feels toward them.

Now by this sign shall ye know the sloppy-minded: that they will jump the guns on exhaustive investigation and substitute certitude for certainty. And that in the light of the literal fact, which Justice Holmes has made into maxim for the law, the simple fact that "certitude is never the test of certainty." Nothing logical whatsoever, that is, follows from the fact that anyone is filled with certitude about anything. Such is too rigorous a rule, however, as we have said, by which to judge the generality in politics. There all but the opposite idea prevails: claim everything in sight. Be like Chanticleer: the cock crowed; the sun came up; nobody else claimed credit for sunrise — Chanticleer carried off the honors. It was clear enough to Chanticleer that he brought the sun up — for he crowed and up it came! — and he got by with it among the hens. So his certitude, motivated by his natural cockiness, prevailed as certainty. But that was in the barnyard.

Lincoln, however, was not of the barnyard; he lived in the sunlight of spirit. He was a man with a mind more scrupulous than it is wise to expect outside of science. The more honor to him, servant as he also was of truth.

Note, finally, how he works the matter out, saving himself from the pitfall of presumption:

> I am naturally anti-slavery [observed Lincoln of his deepest moral self]. If slavery is not wrong, nothing is wrong. I cannot remember when I did not so think and feel.

There Lincoln clearly reveals the stuff of which certitude is mostly made: feelings enkindled in childhood and fed with the provender of custom and enhanced by the osmosis of sympathy. Lincoln probably saw negro slaves sold on the block at New Orleans; we know what at least he is reported to have said about it. Still, for all his personal certitude against its wrongness, he goes on to say:

> Yet I have never understood that the Presidency conferred upon me an unrestricted right to act officially upon this judgment and feeling. . . . And I aver that, to this day, I have done no official act in mere deference to my abstract judgment and feeling on slavery.

Slavery is not the only illustration in Lincoln's life, though it would appear crucial enough, of this fine-edged scrupulosity. I believe no other public man ever lived, certainly none in America, who kept so constantly in mind, and so often let slip into formal utterance, such overtones of logical rectitude. Typical is the concluding sentence of the speech at Cooper Union, which sent him speeding toward the White House: "Let us have faith that right makes might, and in that faith let us to the end dare to do our duty *as we understand it.*" [3] That qualifying phrase, inserted against all the need for oratorical emphasis, is as

---

[3] Italics mine.

conclusive as it is concluding. Here was a statesman who even into the field of politics carried, to a degree not elsewhere matched, the double-entry bookkeeping so honorable to science: of what one *believes* and of what one *knows*. It is Lincoln's service of an ideal which in the conventional division of labor was not his own, nor even his responsibility — the ideal of Truth — that reinforces Lincoln's title to an apostleship in the spiritual life of mankind. Nor was he lacking distinction in still the third dimension of spirit, in the service of Beauty.

Lincoln as a Natural Artist, Serving Beauty

To do justice, however, to Lincoln's servitude to Beauty, we must attain the level where this ideal achieves full stature. We must rise from the purely perceptual to the conceptual, from the personal locus to the social configuration. It is not that beauty does not have its sensuous side, its subjective aspect; and not that these are unimportant. Nor yet is it that Lincoln did not add to the ledger of Beauty on all levels. No one can take the full measure of fitness in illustrations which Lincoln indulged, nor the complete aptness of his homely stories for bodying forth things universal, without seeing that even over the humblest things Lincoln from youth spread the mantle of imagination, transfiguring into something uncommon every common thing. His style — always a subtle measure of the man — irradiates whatever it touches. Even logic Lincoln makes aesthetic, as in the famous letter to Greeley, which we shall presently quote to this and to larger account. "Four score and seven years ago" — that is a poet in the boots of a statesman sludging his way up Olympus. Lincoln's gentility in dealing with men, his withdrawals, his utter disinclination to foist his certitude upon others as certainty (which we have commemorated as also sensitivity to Truth), and in general his will not to intervene in other people's business or suffer from others any presumptuous intimacy (few people, if even his wife, called his given name to his face), and in a word his sustained and eloquent reticence — this all is but visible fitness in overt affairs, prologue to more subtle forms of artistry. So much for the sensuous, the personal, and the perceptual dimensions of beauty, present for all to see in Lincoln's life.

But these are not the final forms, and so

not the ultimate test, of aesthetic aptitude. There is another pattern that appropriates all these and turns them to final account. There is a beauty interpersonal which illustrates the artist's final vision. Not the simplicity that is this side of the complex but that which lies on the other side — as Justice Holmes has happily suggested — that is the simplicity which is genius, no less aesthetic than ethical. Life, as the same sagacious judge has said, "is painting a picture, not doing a sum."

It is this ultra-dimension of beauty which Goethe celebrates at the end of his *Faust*. Recall the magnificence of the pattern which he traces. The forces of nature have been subdued to the service of man. Man has been adjusted to man, as well as to nature, in such wise that peace can maintain itself through perpetual self-renewal. The pomp of ceremony, the calming hand of tradition, and the spritely variety bodied forth by free men freely living together — this is a picture which transcends, while containing, all simpler forms of beauty.

>   . . . could I but stand
> With a free people, and upon free land!
> Then might I to such moment of delight
> Say, "Linger with me, thou that art so
>   bright!"

Such configurative consummation has
been the conscious goal of the aestheticians
as of the practicing poets and painters. Plato began, and in statement climaxed, this
tradition at the very prime of our Western
world. Working up from the particular,
the sensuous, and the personal, this Greek
in his immortal dialogue, the *Symposium*,
allows Socrates (coached by a woman how
to complete and to universalize artistic
diversity) to state what is the aesthetic
finality of the most robust souls: to "see the
beauty of institutions and laws, and to
understand that the beauty of them is all
of one family." To one who has disciplined
himself for the final view, the vision of
"a single science of beauty everywhere," to
him comes the ultimate aesthetic discovery,
namely, as Plato has it, that "the greatest
and fairest sort of wisdom is that which
is concerned with the ordering of states

and families" — a form of beauty which, as he adds, is "called wisdom and justice."

With that norm grasped, as from a master — yea, two masters, Goethe and Plato — let us return to Lincoln, the aesthetic neophyte of the frontier, to see how spiritually robust he was as touching Beauty. By accident there early fell into Lincoln's hands Blackstone's *Commentaries* on the common law. This was the medium through which at one literary leap Lincoln cleared in youth the distance, as Plato prescribes, from "love of one or a few beautiful bodies" to a firm fixation upon institutions and laws. This vision added perturbation but also depth to Lincoln's character. As a neighbor he saw families rent asunder, as he had felt intermitted, through a broken engagement, his own aspiration for intimate union. But the vision never forsook him of an affinity of men and women in self-fulfilling unison. He saw at the bar rents disfiguring the fabric of community and corporate unity, but the ideal of a healing justice informed his legal practice and permitted him to see both sides of

issues in controversy — both sides indeed
of even the national disunion. "If all
earthly power were given me," says he of
slavery, "I should not know what to do
[about it]." Meantime, he would return
fugitive slaves to the South, and would
not sit in harsh judgment upon Southerners
for doing what Northerners, said he, would
have done.

Lincoln dreamed at night, and from
youth, of a mighty nation marching not in
lock-step but to the beat of a common
thought, from triumphs in sympathy to
climaxes of justice. This vision became a
part of him, stirring his fears, informing
his hopes, and harnessing all his creative
energies. It supplanted everything else as
a motive; it became what his friend in
Congress — though later his enemy in war
— what Alexander Stevens called "the sub-
limity of a religious mysticism." This vision
of union led him through the wilderness of
life, up the steeps of fratricidal pathos, being for him a pillar of cloud by day, and
a pillar of fire by night.

See how poignantly he puts the overshadowing majesty of union in his immortal letter to Greeley. This letter is an inspired scholium on Plato and a deserving model to all who thirst for Beauty, in her most majestic distillation:

I would save the Union. I would save it the shortest way under the Constitution. If there be those who would not save the Union unless they could at the same time save slavery, I do not agree with them. If there be those who would not save the Union unless they could at the same time destroy slavery, I do not agree with them. My paramount object in this struggle is not either to save or destroy slavery. If I could save the Union without freeing any slave, I would do it; and if I could save it by freeing all the slaves, I would do it; and if I could save it by freeing some and leaving others alone, I would also do that. What I do about slavery and the colored race, I do because I believe it helps to save the Union; and what I forbear, I forbear because I do not believe it would help to save the Union. I shall do less whenever I shall believe what I am doing hurts the cause, and I shall do more whenever I shall believe doing more will help the cause.

The logical chastity of this letter — its concentration of attention, its amplitude of conception, its economy of diction — is all brought to a climax by the arresting beauty of the theme that held his thought as he penned the reply to Greeley, who had accused him in substance of not knowing what he was about. The Lincoln who did not claim to have "directed events," who indeed confessed that he had been "directed by events," this Lincoln never admitted any lack of *self-direction* or any absence of a guiding vision. Duty without beauty is meager and thin, and insufficient as a motive force; but beauty *and* duty make the world to shine. Ethics climaxed by aesthetics, that is our saving formula; for it represents character in the service of vision. Lincoln did not claim always to know the way, but the direction he never missed. He had seen the loveliness of unity, and in that sign he knew he was to conquer. Early in life vows were made, not so much by him as for him, which rendered Lincoln, like Wordsworth,

> . . . else sinning greatly,
> A dedicated spirit . . .

If he had been himself a poet, instead of a lay custodian of the poetry of life, he could, as truly and as nobly as Wordsworth, have declared of himself:

> Never did I, in quest of right and wrong,
> Tamper with conscience from a private aim;
> Nor was in any public hope the dupe
> Of selfish passions; nor did ever yield
> Wilfully to mean cares or low pursuits.

With what appears an unprecedented combination of the "push" of duty and the "pull" of beauty, Lincoln's iron determination was always being diverted by kindness, but the vision which he had seen toughened his mercy with an adamant will. Preceding and conditioning his magnificent utterance — "With malice toward none; with charity for all" — Lincoln makes poignantly clear in his Second Inaugural that if the alternative is sacrifice of this beauty-duty ensemble, he would continue the war "until all the wealth piled by the bonds-

man's two hundred and fifty years of un-
requited toil shall be sunk, and until every
drop of blood drawn with the lash shall
be paid by another drawn with the sword."
An absorbing aesthetics gave fiber to a
resolute ethics. Lincoln did not misunderstand, as many liberals misunderstand,
the cost of mercy, the stern constitution
of love. He grasped intuitively what the
contemporary British poet, C. Day Lewis,
has so stridently expressed:

> For love's no laughing matter,
> Never was a free gift, an angel, a fixed
>   equator.
> Love's the big boss at whose side for
>   ever slouches
> The shadow of the gunman: he's mortar
>   and dynamite;
> Antelope, drinking pool, but the tiger
>   too that crouches.
> Therefore be wise in the dark hour to
>   admit
> The logic of the gunman's trigger,
> Embrace the explosive element, learn the
>   need
> Of tiger for antelope and antelope for
>   tiger.

But the vision of institutional beauty also tempered Lincoln's course with wistfulness or pathos, where mercy would have entailed irresolution. This vision of a restored Union was the polestar which held him to his course, irrespective of inner lassitude toward war, and in disregard of the tempest of outer pressures. His First Inaugural describes the goal from which he never wavered, and it was essentially the goal envisaged by Goethe, the goal conceptually immortalized by Plato. See Lincoln fill the canvas with a firm hand:

> I am loath to close [he says at the end of the Inaugural]. We are not enemies, but friends. We must not be enemies. Though passion may have strained, it must not break our bonds of affection. The mystic chords of memory, stretching from every battlefield and patriot grave to every living heart and hearth-stone all over this broad land, will yet swell the chorus of the Union when again touched, as surely they will be, by the better angels of our nature.

That prophecy was delayed of fulfillment, though it proved to be the heir of stern events. Intervening were secession, four bloody years of war, victory for the Union armies, and a long hard pull of patriots on both sides to reunite what the war had severed. Only measurably fulfilled even yet is that prophecy, but enough to keep yearning informed with hope. Meantime the slaves were emancipated but the Negroes were not freed, nor are they yet freed into the equality of opportunity which should inform a great nation's life. Interrupting the joyous events between the last battle of the war and the implementation of Lincoln's sagely developing peace policy, came Lincoln's own assassination, his triumphal occupancy of a lonely tomb in Springfield, and the beginning of his national canonization as America's most saintly personage, "Father Abraham."

At the very doorway of his death, however, an event occurred which I dare, despite its appearing trivial, to make the test of his discipleship to Beauty. To a great crowd, on the forenoon of April 10, 1865, serenading the White House in cele-

bration of Lee's surrender, Lincoln made
this surprising little speech:

> I see you have a band. I propose now
> closing up by requesting you to play a
> certain air, or tune. I have always thought
> "Dixie" one of the best tunes I ever heard.
> . . . I ask the band to give us a good turn
> upon it.

The more one reflects upon the symbol-
ism of that simple enough request, the
more magnanimous the thought and the
more beautiful the act. Who makes a nation's songs makes the nation's souls. Who
captures their songs should be able to win
their souls. As the first act in the flush of
victory, the conqueror proposes to play the
national anthem of the defeated foe. It
is doubtful whether more *noblesse oblige*
was ever intended than was consummated
in this passing event. Such generosity at
the personal level we are well acquainted
with, and in nobody better than in Lincoln.
For instance, to a querulous criticism from
Horace Greeley, he began his famous Union
letter with these marvelous words:

If there be in [your letter] any statements or assumptions of fact which I may know to be erroneous, I do not now and here controvert them. If there be in it any inferences which I may believe to be falsely drawn, I do not now and here argue against them. If there be perceptible in it an impatient and dictatorial tone, I waive it in deference to an old friend, whose heart I have always supposed to be right.

Yes, it is easier at the personal level. But men, generous with individuals, may be adamant with groups, especially to groups but now worsted at war. Such magnanimity as Lincoln's with reference to the song of a fallen foe, the symbol of his spirit — this is indeed a rare thing in the world. The very soul of morality, magnanimity is also the texture of Beauty corporately conceived and configuratively embodied.

Lincoln as a Secular Saint, in Deference to Wholeness

We have brought ourselves at last, by successive intimations, to a fourth ideal, that of Holiness. It is a zenith peculiarly associated with religion. Since our hero, however, was not formally religious, how shall we claim for Lincoln a stake in the Holy, as we have made out his claim to each of the other great ideals? We shall do it by assimilating "holiness" to *wholly-ness,* as Thomas Carlyle long ago leagued the "holy" with the *healthy.* As indeed it is not healthy for a man not to see beyond himself, so the full halo of holiness belongs only to the head of him who acknowledges and defers to the Whole, whether he can positively characterize it or not. Men may apprehend what they cannot compre-

hend, and holy men will orient their lives
with reference also to their apprehensions.
Our holy man will be one with Wordsworth, who

> . . . sees the parts
> As parts, but with a feeling of the whole.

But there are two types of whole here
involved. There is the *whole of value*
which we have been filling in with Truth,
Goodness, and Beauty; and there is the all,
the Whole (which we shall capitalize, not
to deify it but merely to distinguish it). Indeed, whether *the* Whole is to be deified
is one of the open questions to the open
mind. (Else what's faith for?) With reference to the whole of value, we have already
seen Lincoln achieve deference toward
Truth and Beauty, beginning with his own
specialized value-form, Goodness as Justice. Precisely here is the minimum meaning of holiness: that one be respectful of
and tolerant toward the other man's value,
that indeed he reverence the value-whole
rather than merely his part. The maximum

meaning of holiness is that one stand in awe before the Whole, of which he is himself so small a part. The final *un*holiness is that one equate himself with the All, and next to it is the presumption that one dare to speak to others in the name of the Whole. The "holy" attitude toward the Whole we have seen in Lincoln's refusal to make Providence *ex parte*. His holiness shines through his reticence, yea reluctance, to claim all the good for his own side.

Lincoln had seized intuitively what Plotinus and other philosophers have reasoned out as "negative theology": that the only way to speak of the Whole without disrespectfully limiting it, is to say only what it is *not*. The Whole is clearly more than any one of its parts, and it may well be more than all its parts. The part cannot adequately characterize the Whole, because the Whole of which the part speaks is only the part's view of the Whole, which, in turn, is *all* views plus what all views *view*. Modesty before the Whole is therefore the essential attribute of holiness. Whether we give to the Whole the name of God, as many are wont to do, or indicate it more neutrally, the final modesty is, nevertheless, in Job's cry, "Though he slay me yet will I trust in Him!"

The man of supreme holiness — and Lincoln approached this maximum — may even be neutral as between optimism and pessimism as touching the Whole. Man must "accept the universe" whether he likes it or not; so why not achieve the dignity of equanimity? Let us turn to the poets for proper illustration of this before returning to Lincoln as exemplification of Whollyness. He who was temperamentally pessimistic but intellectually optimistic, he will confirm what the poets do teach us: that there is no inexorable logic to dictate as between final optimism and pessimism; that indeed holiness is compatible with any sort of Whole. This is also the lesson of the philosopher of the poets, Spinoza: that it is not the first thing to *like* the universe; the first thing is to *accept* it.

Now one may accept the universe, as Thomas Hardy did, in the realistic spirit of his apology for *Jude the Obscure:* "Truth will be truth alway." Says Hardy in another poem, "The Blow":

That no man schemed it is my hope —
. . . .
And if it prove that no man did,
And that the Inscrutable, the Hid,
    Was cause alone
Of this foul crash our lives amid,
I'll go in due time, and forget
In some deep graveyard's oubliette
    The thing wherof I groan,
And cease from troubling; thankful yet

Time's finger should have stretched to
    show
No aimful author's was the blow.

Or one may accept the universe in something like the opposite fashion, but still with full piety. Tennyson's well-known lines are its classic embodiment:

O yet we trust that somehow good
    Will be the final goal of ill,
. . . .
That nothing walks with aimless feet;
    That not one life shall be destroy'd,
    Or cast as rubbish to the void,
When God hath made the pile complete.

And yet Tennyson's optimism closes with a reticent qualification forgotten or unknown by many who make him their mouthpiece:

So runs my dream: but what am I?
An infant crying in the night;
An infant crying for the light:
And with no language but a cry.

It is this modesty, whether optimistic or pessimistic, which brings us back to our theme: the proper relation of the part to the Whole. Milton it is who has given to us, in fashion uninvidious as between pessimism and optimism, the final statement of spirituality in the mode of the holy:

God doth not need
Either man's work or his own gifts; who best
Bear his mild yoke, they serve him best.

In the enlarged perspective now furnished by the poets, let us turn back to Lincoln, and presently to his kind, for our final lesson. Lincoln did not fall into either the piteous presumption of thinking he was the Whole or the presumption provocative of speaking in the name of the Whole to other men, without the others' consent. War power makes presumption easy. Partisanship over slavery saw black as black and white as white and invoked the Whole to bespeak its *ex parte* shibboleth. Not so Lincoln. He was too honest to circumvent scrupulosity, and the Whole he dealt with was "too vast for malice." In "holy" understanding, he declared of the Southerners with sympathy unsurpassed: "They are just what we would be in their situation. If slavery did not now exist among them, they would not introduce it. If it did now exist among us, we should not instantly give it up."

Knowing that he was not God, Lincoln not only beautifully exemplified modesty in practice, but he gave us also a remarkable illustration in the concrete of what is involved in the distinction between modesty and presumption. It is in the last public address he ever made, an address in celebration of Grant's victory only two days old, and in clarification of his own plan of reconstruction which was already under criticism and was, of course, to be interrupted by assassination only three days afterwards. The entire speech — if you will see it so — turns round the very point we have been discussing: the proper relation, that is, between the part and the Whole, a relation with which we have identified holiness. As we peruse the pertinent paragraphs of his speech, it will become clear that Lincoln is broadening politics out into the metaphysical conviction upon which the Fathers predicated our constitutional separation between church and state — the conviction, in short, that private belief and public action must be kept apart if they are to work together for the common good. He obtrudes the moral that sacred things, final things, are to be appropriated and privately celebrated rather than precipitated and publicly perpetrated.

Now that the Union (his earthly Whole, as we have seen) had been saved, its recovery, he declared, in beginning the speech, was being put in jeopardy by the human will to make an unanswerable question the basis for reconstructive action. This question was, in his own formulation, "whether the seceded States, so called, are in the Union or out of it." That final question, the nature of the patriotic Whole, was for practice unanswerable because in theory it was diversely answered. It had indeed caused the war. Now it was showing its head again, in the North. As Lincoln pointedly puts the matter: ". . . we, the loyal people, differ among ourselves as to the mode, manner, and measure of reconstruction." That is always the trouble with the Whole in relation to action: different parts bespeak a different whole. Co-operation must often forgo the use of capital letters.

I have [says Lincoln, coming to the naked issue] purposely forborne any public expression upon it. As appears to me, that question has not been nor yet is, a practically material one, and that any discussion of it, while it thus remains practically immaterial, could have no effect other than the mischievous one of dividing our friends. As yet, whatever it may hereafter become, that question is bad as the basis of a controversy, and good for nothing at all — a merely pernicious abstraction.

Let us interrupt to remark that this is the inexorable tragedy of the spiritual life, that the other man's dearest dogma becomes usually but "a merely pernicious abstraction" when it gets in the way of our own compulsative efforts — and, let us also add, that it is always getting in the way.

We all agree [continues this wise psychosomatic medicine man] that the seceded States, so called, are out of their proper practical relation with the Union, and that the sole object of the government, civil and military, in regard to those States, is to again get them into that proper practical relation. I believe that it is not only possible, but in fact easier, to do this without deciding or even considering whether these States have ever been out of the Union, than with it. Finding themselves safely at home, it would be utterly immaterial whether they had ever been abroad. Let us all join in doing the acts necessary to restoring the proper practical relations between these States and the Union, *and each forever after innocently indulge his own opinion*[4] whether in doing the acts he brought the States from without into the Union, or only gave them proper assistance, they never having been out of it.

It remains only for us to note carefully *when* and *where* it is "innocent" to assert one's own faith as to finality. This we can see at once, that it is after the hour of action and it is in the privacy of one's own ("each . . . indulge his own") soul. This noted as one's metaphysical home base, we may now extend Lincoln's wisdom into a summary view of the danger which the part always sustains in confrontation with the Whole. That each of us is so confronted is certain and that each of us must risk a commitment with reference to the Whole need not be denied. Shall the risk be that of bold prowess or of "wise passiveness"?

Men going on a journey — and a pilgrimage is a journey — must start *from where they are and go on what they've got.* But where *are* we located, we mortal pilgrims

_____
[4] Italics mine.

headed outward, as we are, toward infinity? We are caught, each one, in his own finitude. Even infinity finitely apprehended, is not infinite but finite. Infallibility as grasped by fallible men, is not infallible but fallible. This, then, is our common location, our joint predicament. Not even by humbly compounding our fallibilities can we beget a corporate infallibility, despite whatever presumption of infallibility is declared in Church, or by State, or through the monstrous misalliance of Church and State. "Oh, why," we may ask with Lincoln, "why should the spirit of mortal be proud?" For that is where we are, each caught as a part in a Whole which at the best we but dimly apprehend. Pride is presumption, reticence is reverence, in the presence of the All.

An Evaluation of the Three Values as Approaches to the Value - Whole

There is little likelihood, however, that men can exemplify modesty toward the Whole of Being who have not even managed magnanimity toward the whole of value. So let us leave the larger until we can master the lesson of the smaller. Men must grow from more to more if more of reverence in them is to dwell. How, then, do we go forward toward value cosmopolitanism from the value provincialism with which we start? We must go on what we've got — or we do not go at all. What we have as given are special value approaches to the whole of value; we have as guides to Ideality itself the plurality of our historic ideals: Truth and Beauty and Goodness. Few of us have learned to tolerate them all, or to use each his special value with full reverence in subordinating any two to any one of them without depreciating the two. Yet our technological division of labor is matched by an ideal division of labor; and so different ones of us find ourselves, willy-nilly, as artists approaching the value-whole in the name of Beauty; as scientists in the name of Truth; and as citizens in the name of Goodness. The specialized approach may become as fruitful as it is inevitable; but it is not divorced from danger, nor is the danger to be mastered without discipline. The danger involved mounts steadily as the option moves from Beauty to Goodness, and climaxes itself as choice fixates upon Truth as spirit's most perilous path toward maturity of spirit.

Beauty is the least hazardous, and the most fruitful, of our specialized ideals in the name of which to advance toward the whole of value, that half-way house on the way to the Whole of Being. "Beauty," says Plato truly, "is certainly a soft, smooth, slippery thing, and therefore of a nature which easily slips in and permeates our souls. For I affirm that the good is the beautiful." Whether the two be one or not, it is easiest in the name of Beauty to come to the forbearance which declares, with Kipling, that

> There are nine and sixty ways of con-
> structing tribal lays
> And—every—single—one—of—them—is—
> right.

The mediation of Beauty accommodates a Goodness that is gracious and a Right that is roomy enough to condemn no honest effort as really wrong. Not so easy but still not impossible is it to come through Goodness to the mollifying influence of Beauty (they are of the same family, says Plato) so that the whole need not be ugly, and also through Goodness to come to a Truth that at least is not fanatical enough to damn any earnest effort as mortal error. But Truth, we must repeat, is the most austere of the ideals, and yet the commonest reliance, as conductor to the value-whole if not indeed on to *the* Whole itself.

How parsimonious Truth is as a guide to Wholeness, may be seen in the all too common judgment that "everything is either true or false." Any such brittle distinction between light and darkness serves chiefly the darkness. It is ordinarily made only by those who, in sharpness of spirit, have many whom they would consign to darkness. Witness hereunto the stark companion judgment that "there are many ways of being wrong but only one way of being right." Let us inspect these two companion pieces as obstacles to the attitude which we are willing to call "holy."

Certain it is that not everything has to be either true or false. Few things are either true or false. Most things indeed are *neither* true *nor* false. They may, the rather, be beautiful or ugly, good or bad, useful or useless. If ideality has to be particularized into different ideals — and history has left us no choice — then we must honor the differentiation, and not permit one division of the immense load of ideality to carry all the precious burden. Truth is not all — though, as George Santayana says, "to covet truth is a very distinguished passion."

It is the tragedy of the spiritual life that it is just this ideal of Truth, the most dangerous ideal, upon which Western man has seized, and does now fasten, in order to reduce ideality that is plural to a monistic and manageable proportion. So much so that the most clairvoyant philosopher of our time, George Santayana, has in his apprehension over this matter given us warning by denominating this logical truncation of value "the tragic realm of truth."

A cure, however, may be compounded for this tragedy, and Lincoln is our national apothecary. In compounding his formula' for life and health, Lincoln honored a distinction between "true" and "Truth" which can save us, as it saved him, from unideal sharpness in the name of ideality. Let us put it plainly: the single term "truth" has come to have two different and at time incommensurable meanings. It sometimes means a specific belief that is proved, and it sometimes means a cluster of beliefs that a man or a like-minded group of men prefer as a way of life, but a cluster that is incapable of scientific proof. We shall use the adjective "true," where not too awkward, to signify the proved, and at any rate the capitalized "Truth" to signify a preferred faith.

Now this uplifted "Truth" is not true at all, as something demonstrable to all honest and intelligent men. The fact of differences among such men is proof enough of this. So to accommodate with appropriate terms the Truth that is not true, we have "artistic truth" or "religious truth" or, better still, "poetic truth." There is a Truth, as Wordsworth the poet said, that is "not individual or local, but general and operative." It is indeed so "general" that it can never be demonstrated, but it is also so "operative" that no man can do without it, and most men prefer such Truth to the kind that is "true." "Who cares a damn," queries C. Day Lewis, the modern-day Wordsworth —

> . . . for truth that's grown
> Exhausted haggling for its own
> And speaks without desire?

Very precious indeed is this larger meaning, too precious to get hardened by narrowing it confusedly down to what can be demonstrated. Not only does this larger Truth not lend itself to that test, but that test when applied to it ruins all its beauty, investing vision with intolerance and deepening intolerance into persecution. The test of such large Truth is that it need not exclude anything; it is compatible with everything, even with its opposite.

As demonstrable, a belief must of course be either true *or* false. Not so with our uplifted Truth: it is quite compatible with "error." There can be, that is, any number of "Truths" of this sort, without their getting in one another's way, if men will but have it so. An "erroneous" Faith is but the other man's way of seeing or exhibiting his "Truth." All we need to begin with, in order to lay hold upon this all-inclusive Truth, is generosity. Man can begin the conquest of this high value by merely permitting others the right he claims for himself, the right of each to define his own honesty. What begins as bare tolerance of differences (beyond the demonstrable) may end as love of fecund variety. This is a great gain for the spiritual life, for it neither excludes nor mutilates any manifestation of spirit.

Lincoln's historic task was, as he defined it, so to save "the Union as to make and keep it forever worthy of saving." His pedagogical task must be redone each generation, that is, to help save our personal unity by enlarging every man's spirit until he can let all the faithful live while himself living the life of the faithful. To live by the faith of Lincoln is to find room for every Faith. In learning this limitation of the ideal of truth, we have no better teachers than Emily Dickinson in the name of Beauty, and the Sage of Monticello in the name of Goodness. The poet from Amherst matches Lincoln's wistful spirit over the presumption of men, and spreads the mantle of magnanimity over value-sectarianism in these haunting but lethal lines:

I died for beauty, but was scarce
Adjusted in the tomb,
When one who died for truth was lain
In an adjoining room.

He questioned softly why I failed.
"For beauty," I replied.
"And I for truth, the two are one;
We brethren are," he said.

And so, as kinsmen met a night,
We talked between the rooms
Until the moss had reached our lips
And covered up our names.

As for Jefferson's influence, Lincoln's
constant appeal to the Declaration of Independence was motivated in large part
by the expansiveness of that document: not
only is "property" as an end of government
there expanded to include "pursuit of happiness" but that expansive phrase is further
expanded to let each citizen define the
terms for himself, as far as *equal* rights
permit.

With historic perspective, Jefferson had
early seen that unity of Faith is simply
not attainable without the most generous
leeway in any monistic category. The effort

to attain it had, and has, stained the earth with blood, and yet has had no other effect, he thought, than "to make one half the world fools, and the other hypocrites." Perhaps uniformity, which is not attainable, is not even desirable. That was to Jefferson a glad thought which begot the happy analogy that uniformity of opinion is no more desirable "than that of face and stature." Since variety must be accepted, why not accept it graciously and thus transform fate into freedom?

This heroic resolve of Jefferson discloses to us that his historic *act* to separate church and state was accompanied by a secular *faith* which was the Magna Charta of the human spirit along all fronts. It is lucky that we can not only revive his conclusion but re-establish his premises as sectarianism once more raises its head on this issue, which all unsectarian minds thought settled by Jefferson for the unity of America and the peace of the world.

This faith led Jefferson to say that he had "never submitted the whole system of [his] opinions to the creed of any party of men whatever, in religion, in philosophy, in politics, or in anything else where [he] was capable of thinking for [himself]." It led him to declare: "I am for freedom of religion, and against all maneuvering to bring about a legal ascendancy of one sect over another." It enabled him to say of the most crucial religious belief (that between theism and atheism): "It does me no injury. . . . It neither picks my pocket nor breaks my leg." It led him to add, what is rendered no whit less true by all the intervening time, that "History . . . furnishes no example of a priest-ridden people maintaining a free civil government." And it nerved him, fullest testament of all to holiness, to refuse to disclose to the public what his final private beliefs were lest he "betray the common right of independent opinion by answering questions of faith, which the laws have left between God and [the man] himself."

It was this Jefferson who became Lincoln's main teacher as to this all important distinction between the "true" and the "Truth." Lincoln learned the lesson well, as we have seen; and so played the human part of modesty as touching both the value-whole and the Whole of Being. Though it is easier to learn the lesson today than in Lincoln's time, not all men learn it; and those who do so tend constantly to forget it. It is a fairly recent thing, and still a precarious thing, that men are able as a matter of fact to distinguish between the demonstrable and the otherwise desirable. Science has enabled us to know many more things for certain — but not enough, not nearly enough, for most men to live by. Those who take truth as their preferred value and so use it as a norm have, of course, therefore, to extend its meaning from science to an emotional constellation much more general. Now this extension is natural, perhaps inevitable, and may indeed be fruitful if not used to deceive oneself or to abuse others.

To get sufficient beliefs and beliefs satisfactory enough to live by, the term Truth must be made to cover the good (rather than the "true") and to cover the beautiful (rather than the "true"). We say, for instance, that Democracy is our political Truth (meaning that it is a system that is good and beautiful, not that all its propositions can be demonstrated). If we are beguiled into believing that the democratic Faith by which we live is a set of propositions self-evident or even scientifically demonstrable, we will not only never understand our enemies, who scoff at our "proofs," but we will lose our friends in an effort to prove what is indeed dependable enough until we undertake to demonstrate how dependable it is. (Thus Lincoln, above, as to whether the Union were of such a *nature* that the States could, or could not, get out of it.)

We say, by way of further example, that some given religion is the Truth. It may well be so if we know what we mean; but we must not mean that its various tenets are demonstrable, save to those who already believe them. For in truth they are *not* demonstrable, as the presence of a plethora of opposing religions makes manifest. This is what George Santayana means when he says that it is "being ideal rather than true [which] makes religion the head and front of everything." "Religion," he says again, "is poetry which is mistaken for science." If we forget this distinction, we will find ourselves defending the most egregious superstitions as being "so," though they be but poetic parts of a total system of beliefs which selected believers (but not those who believe otherwise) find satisfactory, for other than logical reasons. Ambiguity of title does not establish stable possession. Nor is ambivalence the last word in semantics.

"Suppose we call a mule's tail a leg, does not the mule then have five legs?"

"No," runs the Lincolnesque answer; "calling a tail a leg does not make it a leg — it only makes you a liar."

Science indeed at last makes inexcusable what was once unavoidable. Modern men can more and more know what is *so*. But to conclude that because things are not demonstrably true, they are therefore *false* (bad), is to rule out the best things of life: poetry, and art, and religion — indeed all that is nobly imaginative. To say that everything is true or false is, therefore, to say something that is ignorant and pernicious. But to say that everything is possessed of truth or of *some other value,* this is a very different and a very wholesome saying. It is as different as radiant affirmation is from lean negation, as different indeed as praise is from blame. Science, in turn, though the custodian of the demonstrable, has no monopoly at all upon the spiritual life, which is the life of the spirit in all its amplitude. Science with its truth-as-demonstrable has its authentic corner in the domain of spirit, a heroic if tragic corner. The corner is tragic because so narrowed; but it is heroic because of the magnificent endeavors that go to sustain and extend the domain of the demonstrable.

Men, in general, have no obligation whatsoever to yield up what they have found to be valuable, merely because it cannot be shown to be a certain kind of value, scientific for instance. When truth is the theme, nothing can be more important than that theme; but truth as demonstration is not the theme of all men at any time or of many men much of the time. The beautiful is also precious, and the good. Equally ancient are all three forms of value, and equally honorable. Minimum holiness, as we have said, arises from the proper relationship of man, the part, to the whole of value. The whole of value must include all values, regardless of which one we use as our approach to the value-whole.

If, for instance, in our natural drive to simplify the plurality which value is, we start with the true and end with Truth, we do well. But in doing it, we change the venue. This, too, is permissible, and may be fruitful; but it carries a new responsibility: it commits us to other criteria than the logical. If we pass from a narrow hypothesis that is proved to the broad belief which we prefer but cannot prove, then we must not smuggle in what we have already over-passed, namely, the proof. Ambiguity has its uses, but it is no fit club to bash men over the head with. We must assume, instead, responsibility for the criteria *now* involved in our new and uplifted meaning of the ambivalent term. If truth, that is, is to be made to cover all three of our historic values, then to be true in this new sense our claims must be both beautiful and good. We cannot accept less than we ordered.

Intolerance is neither beautiful nor good, though it masquerade in the name of the proved while turning itself to the service of the utterly unprovable. What is ugly and mean is not true in the enlarged sense of the good and the beautiful, and it is not true in the narrow sense (because it is incapable of proof). We can have it *either* way if we don't insist upon having it *both* ways. Intolerance of Church and persecution of State, though often done in the name of Truth, are the denial of all value, as well as of the special value claimed. Though intolerance be preached by institutions that claim to be holy, intolerance is the final *un*holiness: it is response to a value-whole made thereby less than the values of all its parts. In the retributive economy of nature, it is a fair guess that men persecute others, in the sphere of opinion, out of self-shame for claiming the rewards of scrupulosity when they have paid only for the comforts of credulity. The least we can do to justify such ease for ourselves is to allow other men the equal comfort of their own brand of belief. Permissibility for self is involved in, and indeed derives only from, the interpermissibility of opposing convictions. When one is not willing to allow the logical laxity which he claims, he projects his meanness onto others as heterodoxy and proceeds toward compulsion. As orthodoxy can never demonstrate its Truth in the scientific sense, it forfeits what it claims in the moral sense when it fails to meet the moral criterion of generosity. In claiming a value which it does not possess, orthodoxy loses the value it might possess, the beauty and goodness of magnanimity. The moral is that there is no heresy in the life of the spirit. The final faithlessness is to hold any human Faith in error.

But let us spell this abstract analysis out now in a concrete example. We take a case exotic enough not to offend our Christian sectarians and yet indigenous enough to human nature to expose to all the unholiness of both sacerdotal and totalitarian presumption when it seeks to monopolize for its value-part the whole of value.

Ibn Tamurt invested the Spanish city of Cordova in Mediaeval times, demanding death for all Jews (as St. Thomas of the same period invoked death against his own preferred heretics) if they did not immediately proclaim their conversion to Mohammedanism. "It is because I have compassion on you," he assured their supplicating elders, "that I command you to become Muslim; for I desire to save you from eternal punishment." When they pleaded with him further, and even invoked the lethal fruits of their "heresy" to fall upon their own heads, not his, he reaffirmed his edict in the universal idiom of piety poisoned with power, and closed the dire colloquy in these classic words: "I do not desire to argue with you, for I know you will argue according to your own religion."

Thus to ignore criteria, confuse categories, and corrupt the soul does not make emotional Truth logically true; it only makes meanness apparent through all the disguises of historic holiness. The presumption of a value-part to speak in the name of the value-whole is the very denial of the spiritual which constitutes the danger of all religions, and which, even more, becomes the outright curse of every proselyting religion in the world, down to and including communism.

The Final Lesson:
Ideological Magnanimity

It was in the contrary spirit that the sad man of Illinois stood before the moral issue of slavery. He knew it wrong, if anything was wrong; but that did not make it right for him to invoke against it the Whole, when slavery too was a part of the Union. Lincoln had to accept the universe as he found it, however he felt toward it and whatever he would have done had he been God at the prime. If we mortals are to have peace at home, we must live in the light of the Whole. If we are to go somewhere away from home, we must start where we are; start where we are and go on what we have. Lincoln did not feel called upon to do anything about what clearly lay outside his power, though as his power increased, his authorization for action against slavery also increased. (It was abolished not as of moral right but as of military necessity.) Acceptance of his part under fidelity to the whole, this led him to distinguish between a truth that is true and "Truth" that is merely precious; between certitude, which belonged to him as a part, and certainty, which belongs in religion to God, in science to the consensus of the competent, and in politics to a majority fairly constituted.

Yet men who cannot *be* God, can and in a certain sense must *play* God. Lincoln thought that there was a field — of pure individual privacy — where each man could, as he put it, "forever innocently indulge his own opinion" as to the *why* and the *wherefore* of what has nevertheless to be accepted. The private and the public are forever at odds. This is the tragedy of spirit fleshly embodied: that its vision be depreciated in action and its perfection be forever squandered on itself. But this tragedy, once courageously contained, imparts

[91]

light to life, progress to action, and turns
grief to glory. With William Wordsworth:

> Here must thou be, O Man!
> Power to thyself; no Helper hast thou
> here;
> . . . .
> The prime and vital principle is thine
> In the recesses of thy nature, far
> From any reach of outward fellowship,
> Else is not thine at all.

Within the premises of this duality —
where the Right of right-minded men is so
roomy that nobody who seeks it can be
wholly wrong — this self-reliant modesty is
the wisdom of all who are not presumptuous enough to confuse themselves with the
Microcosm of Value or even with the
Macrocosm of Being. This is a wisdom
turned to national counsel by Ralph Waldo
Emerson — but only after he had freed
himself of the sectarianism of the least sectarian of American religious fellowships:
"It is easy in the world to live after the
world's opinion; it is easy in solitude to
live after our own; but the great man is he
who, in the midst of the crowd, keeps with

perfect sweetness the independence of solitude." This is the wisdom of Justice Holmes' counsel — imported in "all sadness of conviction" — "that to think great thoughts [men] must be heroes as well as idealists."

This private apprehension of the Whole, but the quiet and heroic grace to appropriate for action only the role of a part, is that "more" of value (intimated at the beginning) which the religious often lack but so deeply require to render them fully spiritual. They must yield their monopoly if they are to retain their autonomy. The spiritual life, let us finally repeat, is the life of the spirit. This allowed largeness is the "more" which we have attributed to secularity so high that it never forgets that the parts are in the Whole, not the Whole in the parts. If anybody speaks for the Whole, the Whole will do the speaking. If anybody must take care of anybody, the Whole must take care of itself — and, if it be so, of the parts as well.

It was the possession of just this "more" which Jefferson indicated in saying: "I tolerate with the utmost latitude the right of others to differ from me in opinion. . . . I know too well the weakness and uncertainty of human reason to wonder at its different results." It was the possession of this "more" which Jane Addams betokened in warning us "against doing good to people. . . . One does good, if at all," she adds, "*with* people, not *to* people." It was the presence of this "more" that yielded in Lincoln, finally, a holiness compatible with healthiness and constituted of his modesty and reverence a lasting American symbol of man's loftiest spiritual life. But let this secular saint preside at his own canonization through the vivid pertinence of certain points from his Second Inaugural:

> Both parties [said he of the South and of the North] deprecated war; but one of them would make war rather than let the nation survive; and the other would accept war rather than let it perish. . . .
>
> Both read the same Bible, and pray to the same God; and each invokes His aid against the other. . . .
>
> The prayers of both could not be answered — that of neither has been answered fully. . . .

With malice toward none; with charity for all; with firmness in the right, as God gives us to see the right, let us strive on to finish the work we are in; to bind up the nation's wounds; to care for him who shall have borne the battle, and for his widow, and his orphan — to do all which may achieve and cherish a just and lasting peace among ourselves, and with all nations.